THE SKILL

*The Most Critical Tool Needed to Increase Your
Potential, Performance and Promotability*

LES WOLLER

WITH

JAMES WOLLER

Co-authored by: James Woller
Edited by: Amanda Regier
Cover Design / Artwork by: Melanie Cooper

Note for Librarians: A cataloguing record for this book is available from Library and Archives Canada at www.collectionscanada.ca/amicus/index-e.html

Printed in Victoria, BC, Canada.

ISBN: 978-1-4251-6619-9

We at Trafford believe that it is the responsibility of us all, as both individuals and corporations, to make choices that are environmentally and socially sound. You, in turn, are supporting this responsible conduct each time you purchase a Trafford book, or make use of our publishing services. To find out how you are helping, please visit www.trafford.com/responsiblepublishing.html

Our mission is to efficiently provide the world's finest, most comprehensive book publishing service, enabling every author to experience success. To find out how to publish your book, your way, and have it available worldwide, visit us online at www.trafford.com/10510

 www.trafford.com

North America & international
toll-free: 1 888 232 4444 (USA & Canada)
phone: 250 383 6864 ♦ fax: 250 383 6804 ♦ email: info@trafford.com

The United Kingdom & Europe
phone: +44 (0)1865 722 113 ♦ local rate: 0845 230 9601
facsimile: +44 (0)1865 722 868 ♦ email: info.uk@trafford.com

10 9 8 7 6 5 4 3 2

ENDORSEMENTS

Insight into the selection and development of strategic talent – those that make a difference in organizations that create customer and economic value – is critical. The Skill provides unparalleled understanding for individuals and organizations to build the capacity to learn, grow and contribute now. The Skill can be used as a toolset to make giant steps forward in building the potential, performance and promotability of the talent bench. Les Woller has provided the basics for new analytics to measure the identification and accelerated development of talent.

> **— Richard W. Beatty**
> Professor of HR Management,
> University of Michigan and
> Rutgers University, coauthor of
> The Workforce Scorecard

Now more than ever we can see how adapting to change will create success. Whether a recent graduate, seasoned employee or individual working towards self improvement, The Skill delivers a new tool kit for progressing from self awareness to lasting change. Les and James have truly created a manual for success in today's changing world!

> — **Ryan Benn**
> President and Publisher,
> Alive Publishing Group Inc.

This is the "how to" book for all of us working to be better than who we are today. It shows you how to improve your self awareness and then how to change your behavior to be more effective. The specific steps are the most helpful instructions I've ever received.

> — **Ruth Bennett**
> Chief Operating Officer, Bonneville
> Power Administration (Ret.)

For more than 20 years, Les Woller has used The Skill to help business executives learn, grow and succeed. Its four-step methodology is needed and necessary, and it's a process anyone can grasp by reading Les's excellent book.

> — **Ram Charan**
> Consultant and co-author of the best
> selling book *Execution*

As a professional who often provides feedback, the ARTT methodology has given me an effective framework to help individuals make improvements and then sustain them. As a parent of pre-teens, I can also teach the skill to my kids and help them improve their lives. This short book has an impressive amount of value packed into it. It provides an important "secret" to success in today's marketplace and a methodology to help anyone better thrive in today's world.

— **Jillian Dorman**
Former Sr. Manager Sun University,
Sun Microsystems and Principal,
Talent and Performance Strategies

It's seldom true that a book can actually help someone have a more successful career and a better life, but this one can. The Skill is a research based and experience tested self help book about the magic bullet of success - learning agility. What is it and how can I get better at it. A must read for any career minded person.

— **Robert W. Eichinger**
Vice Chairman, KornFerry International
and Cofounder, Lominger Limited, Inc

Les Woller has worked with managers, executives, and leadership teams from well-known corporations for over 30 years. He's "been there, done that"—he knows his stuff. When I need on-target business advice or career help, I go to Les Woller. Now you can too, because he's packed his 30 years of battle-tested experience into a simple, easy-to-use volume: *"The Skill."* Get a copy. Read it. Leap forward.

— **William S. Frank**
Founder and CEO, CareerLab

Over the years, I have witnessed the power of ARTT in action. People change in profound ways. They learn to learn and to improve! They learn how to gain new insights from their everyday successes and failures. I have observed Les' strong ability to understand human behavior. He also has a vast knowledge of psychology and has simplified the essence of how individuals adapt and grow. ARTT is simple, but profound. ARTT is the $E=MC2$ for personal improvement.

— **John Hirsch**
Former Chief Human Resource Officer,
Battelle, Pacific NW Laboratories

Today in my work as board member for several Fortune 500 companies, the perspective I take on my current business challenges has changed. The early insights I gained from Les remain relevant and viable. As I reviewed chapters of *The Skill* I had to smile, because he is now sharing his insights with a broader audience, with even greater clarity. He is a great coach! Thank-you Les.

— **Donna James**
Former President Nationwide Strategic
Investments and Managing Director,
Lardon & Associates

During a time of major transformation , Les' understanding of leadership and coaching expertise played a key role in helping us manage a "smooth" process that met our goals. His book is a readable, practical, how-to road-map on taking responsibility for your own development. It's a Winner!

— **Carl Liebert**
CEO, 24 Hour Fitness

For years my organization has been struggling with developing people in a way that enables people to cope with the accelerating pace of change and complexities as well as higher standard of expectations using formal education, coaching, mentoring, stretch assignments, etc. When I read about The Skill it resonated within me as the way to proceed at both a personal and organizational level. Its wisdom is so self evident. To succeed it requires personal commitment and introspection – constant learning. I will be buying copies of this book to share in my organization!

— **Chris Mazurkewich**
COO, Strategic & Corporate Services,
Interior Health British Columbia, Canada

We are in a new era of change and complexity, especially in the business world. We have to adapt to the times and people often have difficulty making the shift. Les and James Woller offer us an excellent tool and set of principles for every person who has struggled to make the shift. In the end, you will grow, adapt, and continue to learn.

— **Michael McAdam**
President and CEO, Teldon Media Group

Les Woller brought a unique combination of deep experience and insight into our company at a time of extreme change. He provided a common sense approach and process that helped our key leaders navigate a change in ownership, together with changing to a performance-based culture, while remaining focused on the safety of our employees and the satisfaction of our customers. The Skill lays out the elements of a change process that leads not just to change but to results.

— **Frank McShane**
COO, Longview Fibre Paper & Packaging, Inc.

Les' ARTT coaching methodology works. Over the years, it has made a big impact on my life and my career.

— **Curt Nonomaque**
CEO, VHA Inc.

The Skill is a brilliant guide to finding and implementing sound ideas that can be contextualized into every arena of life. The concepts applied, change the course of business performance, but more importantly, positively transform people and entire organizations in the process. This is a timeless and enormously useful book. If you want to keep getting better every day, buy this fresh and inspiring well-written book, study it and keep talking about it with your colleagues.

— **Doris Olafsen**
Vice President, Advancement, Opportunity International

Les Woller has a unique clarity of vision, ability to diagnose and recommend courses of action for personal and professional matters. For over 15 years, I have been engaged in complex conflict resolution through international facilitation and mediation in the Middle East. The guidance and discussions with Les has been invaluable. He is one of the very few people that is able to analyze complex problems and offer strategic and practical solutions.

— *Professor Dr. Scient* **Jon Martin Trondalen**
CEO & Chairman of Compass Foundation, Geneva, Switzerland and Founder of the International Water Academy, Oslo, Norway

The Skill is based on research and practical experience providing readers with a grounded guide to personal development. Many leadership development experts primarily focus on the diagnostic phases of development, however, *The Skill* provides specifics "how-to's" that ensure personal growth. This well-written book provides a rigorous, practical, step-by-step approach to the process of development planning and execution. It is elegantly simple! I know I'll be using *The Skill* and the ARTT model in my teaching at Duke and my own international practice.

— **Randall P. White, Ph.D.**
Principal, Executive Develop Group, Adjunct Professor, Duke Corporate Education and Author of *Relax, Its Only Uncertainty*

To Mary Lee, the love of my life. And to all our children, Joel, Mike, Tracy and James - who are my gifts from God.

This book would not been possible without the drive, determination, and discipline of our son James. It was his organizing skills, experiences, and heart that inspired me to complete the book. There are no words to adequately express my gratitude, respect and love.

Les Woller
2008

"Mama may have, Papa may have but God bless the child that's got his own that's got his own."

— Song lyrics from Billy Holiday
(1936)

CONTENTS

"Nothing endures but change"

— Heraclitus 540 B.C.

FOREWORD

The Skill is a book about change. But, it is not about a short term, fad drive, quick fix change that permeates our lives. It is about fundamental and deep change based on learning. Change tied to the Skill does not begin with dazzle, then fizzle. When people and organizations know and implement ARTT (Aware, Reflect, Target, and Try) they learn what they do, why they do it, how to improve, and how to start. These principles apply to both individuals and organizations.

I appreciate personal change. For years, once or twice a month someone in a seminar would approach me after the workshop and offer personal advice on how I could lose weight. Doctors would diagnose my symptoms as being tied to my weight. I made jokes about it. I knew I should change for personal and social reasons. But, I could not do it. I lived in denial, not facing the reality of my weight problem.

When I finally came to the personal position of making a lifestyle, not just weight change, I followed the steps in the Skill. I made myself Aware of the problem. This meant daily weigh-ins, looking in mirrors, and learning about the risks of extra weight. I Reflected on why I was doing what I was doing. I thought about why and when I used food and exercise. I realized that food played a significant emotional support for my ups and downs. I Targeted specific things I would do to make a lifestyle change. I tracked exercise, carbs, and weight. And then, I Tried to change with specific actions.

In the process of losing weight I learned. And, by learning, I became more disciplined at turning what I knew (eat less, eat right, exercise more) into what I did. Now, three years later, I still struggle with the lessons I learned. After a cruise where I did the inevitable of gaining a pound a day, I had to go back to the same disciplines: being Aware of how I was doing (weigh daily even when I did not want to), Reflect on why it happened (make unconscious choices conscious), Target specific goals, and Try unique actions.

If these four principles work for me in making successful personal change, they also will work for people in organizations who want to change. Some individuals want to be more responsive to their employees and customers; others want to demonstrate better technical skills; others want to communicate more effectively. Regardless of the personal change or organizational change, the four principles in this book will help.

Awareness means that we look in personal mirrors and see the world as it is, not as we would like it to be. We generally can define our strengths, but have a hard time recognizing weaknesses. We often run and hide from things we don't do so well. I recently asked my wife for suggestions on things I should improve, thinking that after 32 years, I would know what she would say. I was surprised that she captured some issues that I probably knew, but denied. Awareness comes from self reflection, but also other connections. We judge ourselves by our intent; others judge us by our behaviors, so we need to be both self and other aware.

Reflection requires thought. Why do we do what we do?

When we understand the Why, we can begin to change the What. Why may include deeper psycho-analysis which uncovers historical patterns. But Why may also include daily antecedents, or prompts which cause us to do some things over others. Reflection is not passively acknowledging why we do what we do, it requires hard thinking and deep understanding of our motives and patterns.

Targeting means goals. Some goals are vision statements of future states. These aspirations engage our minds and hearts. These set a direction in which we are headed and give us a sense of destiny and hope. Other targets are more tangible. They are means to the end; they are measurable, and they are concrete. Targeting requires aspiration and action, direction and discipline.

Trying means we start. Starting small is better than hoping big. Trying does not mean that we succeed, but that we move. Learning from successes and failures enables our trying to lead to progress. When we succeed, we need to gain confidence. When we fail, we need to have resilience. In both successes and failures, we need to learn and improve.

These four principles of ARTT not only apply to personal change, but organizational change. Leaders who want their organizations to change have to be Aware. They have to have honest data about how their organization is working and share that information with those inside and outside the company. Creating a need for change comes from financial, productivity, customer, employee, and other data that reports how the organization is performing.

These leaders then need to Reflect on the data. Reflection allows for interpretation. Leaders want to change patterns not just events. They want to help employees learn why their organization has fallen into dysfunctional patterns, not just offer quick tools to get out. We have used what we call a "virus detector" to help leaders identity underlying viruses in their organizations. When these implicit viruses can be made explicit, they can be changed. Reflection helps with the Why.

Targeting means that organization leaders set both visions for where the organization is headed and goals for how to get there. Targets offer hope and provide measures. Leaders who target well develop employee engagement because employees know how their actions today affect the organization's outcomes tomorrow.

Finally, leaders who change organizations Try. They experiment, continuously improve, seek for best practice, start small, and keep going.

The Skill is not just about change, but about change that endures because it is based on learning. For individuals who want to improve and for leaders who want to transform their organizations, the ARTT principles will work.

Dave Ulrich
Professor, University of Michigan
Partner, The RBL Group (www.rbl.net)

INTRODUCTION

"Faster than a speeding bullet!"

— Radio Catchphrase, Superman (1941)

This book is a response to the breakneck pace of change. As we're sure you know, everything in life is moving faster than it ever has before. Whether you are a CEO, mid-level manager or work for yourself, you've probably been confronted with the change phenomenon. Perhaps you've found your job description being revised not once or twice but three times in the course of a year. Maybe you've gone through a dizzying series of transfers. It may be that your job has been downsized out of existence. And it could be that you are trying to cope with massive new trends in the marketplace.

Whatever your specific experience might be, we're writing this book to equip you with *the Skill* that will help you handle all the career and job issues that change raises. Being able to make transitions to new jobs, bosses, stretch assignments and the like has become the rule rather than the exception for just about

everyone. Unfortunately, most people aren't prepared to make
these transitions successfully.

We've found that a combination of coaching and learning
from experience is the key for doing so. This may sound like
"self-coaching," and to an extent that's an accurate term. But *the
Skill* we're referring to not only is more disciplined and process-
oriented than self-coaching; it has been proven to work. We've
seen too many self-coaching approaches that are overly simplistic
or have little impact on job performance or career goals. *The
Skill* is different. If you want, think of it as "self-coaching *plus.*"
The plus connotes that you're going to receive a lot more than
some friendly advice about how to be more introspective and
reflective. If you can use *the Skill* to understand how you respond to changing circumstances and apply this understanding
to change your behaviors, you can effectively adapt, survive and
thrive. People who master *the Skill* invariably are more effective
in their jobs and more successful in their careers.

We're going to teach you how to acquire and employ *the Skill*
through *ARTT*, a four-step process that we've used with a variety
of people and organizations. First, though, we need to give you a
sense of why we believe you need to acquire *the Skill* now, and why
it will be *the Skill* that separates you from others in the future.

Learning and Adaptability

> We no longer can take our time to learn or enjoy long periods
> where everything stays the same. Today, we are being asked
> to climb steep learning curves with great speed and then adapt
> our behaviors even faster. If we are unable to do this, we won't
> perform well in a job and our career will be limited.

In the next chapter, we're going to focus on the "why now" issue, but here, we want to give you a preview of one of the factors that will compel everyone to master *the Skill*. Think for a moment about what is going to take place in the next five years in terms of the job market. Baby boomers will be retiring in droves—as many as 40% of key jobs may need to be filled. As a result, not only will organizations be under pressure to recruit talent, but to develop that talent at an accelerated pace.

In anticipation of this scenario, organizations are trying all sorts of approaches to help their people develop quickly. For instance, companies have increasingly turned to 360 degree feedback as a tool to raise employee awareness of behavioral weaknesses. This tool is effective in raising awareness—it lets people know what bosses, direct reports and other colleagues think of their work behaviors. While awareness is great, it is only the first step. Unfortunately, most organizations don't help their people take the step beyond awareness to behavioral change. An employee may be concerned about the way he acts in certain business situations and recognizes it is a problem, but he doesn't know how to change. Organizations are increasingly reluctant to spend money on coaches to facilitate that change. In addition, many unofficial potential coaches within companies—bosses, mentors, HR people—are not particularly good at coaching others. Lominger Inc. regularly conducts research to monitor changes in competencies within organizations—what people are getting stronger at versus weaker. In just about every survey, the weakest leadership competency is developing others or coaching.

Another organizational approach is to hire the smartest people they can find. The theory here is that smart people won't have a problem learning and developing talent. In fact, the smartest students often don't make the best, most productive professionals. While straight A students are great learners, they often don't apply that learning in order to change. Thus, they may lack the ability to adapt to changing environments and be effective in more than one set of circumstances.

Learning and adaptability are key elements of *the Skill*. One without the other is not worth much. A great analogy is input and output jacks, the kind you find on a stereo or television. Learning is the input jack—it is how we acquire knowledge. Adaptability is the output jack—it is the process by which we respond to change and apply new behaviors.

When you use *the Skill*, you begin by taking in knowledge about yourself—your strengths and weaknesses as an individual contributor, a manager and so on—and becoming aware of where those weaknesses are tripping you up and why. Using ARTT, many of our clients become conscious of new or changed situations that cause them to act counterproductively, and they start working on ways to adapt their actions so that they become productive.

The ARTT Methodology

ARTT is a four-step process that stands for Aware, Reflect, Target and Try. It involves making yourself Aware of what you are doing in a given situation; Reflecting on why you are acting in a certain way in the situation; setting new behavioral Targets that will yield a more positive result in similar situations; and hitting these targets by Trying new behaviors. (See page 174 for a diagram of ARTT).

We're not going to spend a lot of time now describing the process, since the following chapters will look at each step in detail and provide you with tools such as Self-Talk and an Early Warning System to facilitate the process. Here, though, we want to emphasize that this approach is self-contained, accessible and applicable to any problem or transition you might face.

Once you become comfortable using it, you'll naturally integrate ARTT into your standard operating procedure at work. Rather than having to wait to talk to a coach about a problem you are having or for feedback from a variety of people, ARTT is instantaneous. After some practice, you'll be able to use it in real time, adjusting your behaviors during a presentation or meeting when you become aware that your old approach isn't working.

The process is similar to what occurs during a professional tennis match. During the match, a player can't stop the action every time he hits a bad shot or misses an opportunity for a good one and ask his coach for tips and techniques. He has to play through it and make adjustments on his own if he wants to win. The best players are able to take a figurative step back during a match and observe themselves, recognizing that they are failing to charge the net or are swinging too hard on their forehand. They can immediately translate this awareness into more effective play.

ARTT allows you to learn and adapt in the same way. In the heat of the moment—while trying to make a sale or a point with your boss—you can observe and adjust.

We don't want to make the process sound overly simple or easy. It takes time and practice to become comfortable using ARTT. At first, it may seem a bit awkward to step back and observe both your behaviors and what is going on inside your head. Initially, many people need to reflect on what happened after an event is over, rather than in real time. The good news is that if you are diligent and committed to mastering ARTT, you'll probably be able to use it in real time relatively quick.

To help you attain this mastery, the following chapters will offer you tools and techniques that will allow you to become adept at each of the steps. We'll also provide examples of individuals who have used ARTT to demonstrate what to do-and what not to do.

Why Make the Effort: Career, Job and Organizational Benefits

The odds are that you have plenty of motivation to acquire *the Skill*. Nonetheless, we'd like to share with you the different ways people have benefited from ARTT. As we suggested earlier, ARTT is especially valuable for professionals in fast-changing environments. When you receive a transfer to another country or your organization is acquired, for instance, you are going to face everything from new cultures to new ways of transacting business. These changes often throw people off and they don't fit in anymore. ARTT helps individuals make these transitions with great effectiveness.

Beyond ARTT's ability to help people adapt and deal with change, here are some other ways you may benefit:

✓ Improves your ability to achieve goals

✓ Enhances your performance, potential and promotability

✓ Helps you manage daily stress

✓ Makes it easier to sort through complexity and deal with uncertainty

✓ Improves leadership skills, including ability to network and build trust with colleagues and direct reports

✓ Leads to highly effective decision-making

Without *the Skill*, you will probably struggle in some or all of the bulleted areas. We talk a lot about how people generally operate on autopilot, meaning that they behave and respond to problems and opportunities in unthinking, formulaic ways. As a result, they fall into routines that may have served them well in the past but are no longer effective in a quickly changing environment. That's why they make bad decisions or find it difficult to form productive relationships (especially in a more diverse workforce).

> ARTT allows people to escape their autopilot routines, if necessary, and gives them the chance to develop new and better ways of getting things done.

We should note that these benefits apply whether you are a young executive who wants to be more effective in your job, or a CEO who wants to increase the effectiveness of the entire organization. In our work, ARTT has helped individuals secure promotions to capstone positions as well as enabled top executives to increase their company's profitability simply through making better decisions.

From an organizational perspective, if a critical mass of employees are using ARTT, the effect is transformational. If 5% or 10% of an organization acquire *the Skill*, there is a ripple effect throughout the company. That's because not only are they much more effective leaders, managers and individual contributors, but someone who can use *the Skill* to learn and adapt also makes a great coach of others. More than that, they can pass on Skill-based techniques to their direct reports, helping their people develop and grow.

ARTT, therefore, is a highly versatile tool, one that anyone can become proficient at and benefit from. We know this is true not only from teaching ARTT to clients, but from our own experiences.

How ARTT Evolved

As vice president of executive and organizational development for a large research company, I (Les), was stuck. Though I had achieved a certain amount of success, I was frustrated that I hadn't achieved larger career goals. I recognized that as I became older, my career options were limited and I needed to take action. Yet I felt blocked; I was not sure what to do or how to do it.

During this time, the research organization was growing, and they had hired some of the best and brightest people around. But when these people were placed in leadership positions, many of them were struggling with their transitions. To help them learn faster and more effectively in their new roles, I developed "the learning circle," a process designed to help people learn from their experiences. The learning circle facilitated transitions for these new leaders, and as a result of its success, the company supported my effort to develop an action learning and education program designed to help people deal with organizational change.

Through these efforts, I became fascinated with how people learn and change. More significantly, they helped me test and evolve the process that became ARTT. I was able to use myself as a guinea pig, coaching myself to the point that I became aware of how my behaviors were limiting my career potential; after some reflection, I came to realize that I could only fulfill my career goals as a consultant rather than as an employee.I targeted specific situations where I could test new behaviors and I tried new approaches that turned out to be more satisfying and helped me move closer to where I wanted to be in my career.

The above is a shorthand description of what actually took place. It required months of cycling through ARTT until I was able to leave my company and establish myself as a consultant. Nonetheless, I saw that the process was enormously effective and enabled me to make a transition I had wanted to make for years. Since that time, I've used ARTT to help many professionals in all types of organizations and at all levels. People have told me time and again that ARTT has helped change their lives in the same way it helped change mine. They've found that *the Skill* gives them a way to get unstuck from dead end jobs, to deal with workplace change, to avoid the mistakes and bad decisions that prevent them from advancing and to rise to job and career challenges. Perhaps best of all, it provides them with a way to learn and develop on their own. They aren't dependant on training courses, executive education programs or external coaches. They don't take one step forward when being coached or trained and then two steps backward when they are on their own in the workplace.

Instead, they feel empowered and independent. People often possess far greater capabilities than they give themselves credit for. Under stress, however, they rely on only a small percentage of this capacity. When they're going through transitions or other stressful situations, they lapse into routine behaviors. While these routines are comfortable, they often are not the best ways of getting things done. They don't use approaches that are far more effective, and they are oblivious to how their routines are terribly ineffective.

I know all this not just from observing my clients but because I've gone through life before and after *the Skill*. I experienced a big Aha! when I discovered how ARTT helped me maximize my capacities and achieve quantum leaps in performance.

James, my son, has used *the Skill* since he was 13. Entering into his teens he certainly benefited from his willingness and ability to be self-aware and apply what he learned to adapt his behavior. *The Skill* accelerated the development of his entrepreneurial abilities and by the age of 17 he grew his lawn mowing company to over 135 weekly customers. He subsequently sold the business for a healthy profit. In his final year of university James was elected student body president during a highly volatile time in the university's history. He successfully navigated through key transitions. Next James became the Manager of Strategic Development and Planning for a not-for-profit organization that is rebuilding a community in Africa through the start-up of macro-businesses and urban development.

James continues to use ARTT as it has become second nature to him. ARTT has been *the Skill* which has given him the ability to continually learn, and adapt to new situations and challenges. This has certainly been foundational to his career growth. His insight and understanding of the process has been an inspiration and a key to the development of this book.

ARTT has given me the confidence to believe that I could overcome any obstacle—whether self-created or external—and achieve any objective. I hope that the following pages give you the confidence to achieve your goals as well as a roadmap to get you there.

Chapter i

Why Now? An Era Where *the* Skill Counts

"Can you not discern the signs of the times?"

— Jesus, *The Bible*, Matthew 16:3

The need for *the Skill* is critical today. Without it, even the best and brightest professionals diminish their effectiveness and sabotage their careers. With it, they possess the ability to adapt -a hugely important attribute in a rapidly-changing world. Those who learn to adapt and continue to adapt to changing conditions will be those who are able to successfully navigate through a turbulent world of change.

It has not always been this way. Years ago, it was possible to be successful without a high degree of self-awareness. During a time when people were often "employed for life," worked in relatively stable environments and encountered largely predictable situations, the keys to success were more external than internal. If you were knowledgeable, skilled and diligent, you could be reasonably assured that you'd do well.

The world has dramatically changed since then. Just consider the need for speed, the growing complexity and uncertainty and the pressure for short-term results. For most, stress accompanies almost any significant assignment, whether it's related to tight deadlines, ambitious objectives or stiff competition. In this environment, you must be in touch with what's going on inside of you, not just outside of you. You must be aware if you're relying on a routine autopilot-like process when things become too complicated or if you lapse into a self-protective mode every time a project hits a snag. If you're aware of what you're doing, you can change your behaviors, adapt to the situation and become more effective.

We're going to look at why various work changes make it imperative that people know what is going on inside their heads, not just inside their offices. Combining learning with action to become adaptable is *the Skill* you need to realize your true potential, improve your performance and become more promotable. Before we explain our methodology for acquiring *the Skill*, though, we need to make the case for why it is so necessary for the times in which we live.

The Five Big Trends

If you think back to the world of work in the 1980s, certain words come to mind: stability, predictability, clarity, loyalty. If you fast forward to the business climate today, the words that jump out are: volatility, uncertainty, complexity, speed and ambiguity. Back then, we were a high-production economy, manufacturing a wide range of products. Today, we are primarily a professional services economy; an astonishing statistic is that in 2006, 77% of the US population worked in services, while only 22% worked in industry.

To illustrate the huge gap between what the working environment used to be and what it is now, we have assessed the impact according to five major developing trends, as shown in the following chart:

The 5 Trends	Job Design	Decision Making	Planning	Markets	Workplace
What used to be	• Fairly stable • Organizational structures very similar • Focus on responsibilities	• Centralized at the top • Limited choices • Reasonably paced	• 3-6 month planning periods • Somewhat predictable • Annual updates	• Clear industry groupings • Large markets • Occasional breakthroughs • Market definitions and leaders somewhat stable	• Long term employment • 1-2 locations • Reasonably low turn over • Loyalty rewarded
What is today	• Frequent re-design • Jobs defined by projects and short term results • Very fluid organizational structures • More work being outsourced • The creation of the virtual office	• Participative • High speed • Many choices • Heavy economic pressures	• 2-3 month planning periods • High degree of uncertainty • Many complex variables • Monthly reviews for changes	• Highly segmented • Rapid changes • New competitors • Emerging and unidentified segments • Highly integrated markets	• Geographically dispersed workforce • Many job changes and workshifts • Numerous organizational structure changes • Changes in ownership
Impact	• Frequent change • More career choices • Fewer long-term jobs • Unclear career paths	• Possibility of error is high • The appearance of being inclusive is not authentic • Profit is the driver	• More risks • Little security • Constant change • Difficulty to sustain a strategic direction	• More competitive pressures • Need to market across numerous segments • Need for increased customer awareness	• Increased pressure on time management and family life • Decreased sense of loyalty to organizations • Work locations at home and offshore

For most, this chart strikes a chord—it captures a reality they know all too well. It also highlights the need to adapt to rapidly changing conditions. Let's look at an example that brings the impact of the chart to life. Tim is a 37-year-old sales executive with a Fortune 500 pharmaceutical company. He is the head of a sales team that is responsible for a group of blood pressure-lowering drugs, and during the past year, Tim has been struggling to meet the objectives set for his group. Part of the problem has been an incredibly competitive market, including a highly successful direct-to-consumer television ad campaign run by a competitor. In addition, his company has had to weather negative publicity about one of their products, and even though it wasn't one that Tim was responsible for, the bad press hurt his group's sales. Trying to meet his objectives, Tim has been spending more time in the office and on the road, which has created tension at home—his wife is upset at the long hours he is working.

Tim is also struggling with internal changes at his organization. For one thing, a new CEO came in about a year ago and implemented a number of new programs and policies—ones involving knowledge management and information technology systems--that have had a dramatic impact on Tim's workstyle. He has to spend a considerable amount of time sharing information with other sales groups around the world via the company's intranet site, and he resents having to reveal what he considers his "trade secrets" about selling. Even more troubling is Tim's new boss, who Tim believes has set the bar far too high. This boss also has come from a different company and is obsessive about short-term results. She doesn't appreciate all of Tim's accomplishments, and her abrasive style is at odds with the company's family-oriented culture.

Stressed out by all this, Tim is even more upset when his boss tells him that she's combining his group with two others to increase its "variety and innovation potential." Tim argues with her about this and other approaches, but soon he simply complains about her to his people. Tim also finds himself distracted at work and unable to display the energy and commitment he demonstrated in the past. Normally an even-tempered type of person, Tim has started snapping at direct reports and having less patience with customer requests or complaints. Tim rationalizes his behaviors as being a reaction to stress. When a colleague with whom Tim is close suggests he should talk to someone in human resources about his struggles, Tim brushes the suggestion aside, saying that it's not a big deal.

Adaptability Versus Autopilot

Of course, it is a big deal. Tim, like a lot of professionals, is functioning on autopilot. When people are on autopilot, they fly through their daily decisions without really thinking consciously. Their responses to any given situation are controlled by events that took place in the past. Rather than taking a step back, and gaining perspective before deciding what to do, they are at the mercy of their conditioned responses.

For instance, your boss suggests you might want to try a new way of dealing with a problem, and you *automatically* respond defensively. By relying on a conditioned response, you limit your options for dealing effectively with a given situation. Just as significantly, you prevent yourself from learning anything new. Because you are on autopilot, you lack the awareness to understand what is happening inside of you, and therefore you also lack the adaptability to choose a behavior that's different from your knee-jerk response and appropriate to the situation at hand.

Self Awareness gives you the ability to switch off of autopilot. It provides you with a process to pause, reflect, ask questions for clarification and problem-solve. As a result, you generate a variety of response options, at least one of which will be much more effective than your conditioned response.

Think about the previous scenario for a moment. Imagine your boss offering you constructive criticism, and you end up reacting defensively. What caused you to switch to autopilot? Emotions of which you were not aware. At some point in your past, you received criticism (perhaps from a parent) that you felt was unfair, and you reacted defensively. It may well have been a pattern from your childhood. Now, when your boss criticizes you, those old emotions emerge and switch on your autopilot.

Autopilot has always been a detriment to careers and productivity, but it had less of a negative impact years ago. Back then, if you worked hard, produced quality work and used the same basic skill set to solve problems, you usually did well. Today, these behaviors alone won't even keep you employed, let alone help you get ahead. Today, success is predicated on handling continuous change, working with great speed and leveraging a diverse network. Years ago you didn't have to be particularly aware and adaptable; you could work hard or use the same skill repeatedly and do okay. Today, if you are not aware and adaptable, continuous change will throw you for a loop. If you can't adapt your approach when your organization is flattened or acquired, when you are asked to work globally or virtually, then you are out of luck and probably out of a job. Today, job security is only possible if you're adaptable. Those who can handle change well and shift their approach as situations demand it are highly valued. They've made themselves marketable not because they learn new skills, but because they possess the one *Skill* that allows them to work at peak capacity in the wake of change.

Now let's examine an even more compelling reason for acquiring *the Skill* and becoming adaptable: the Age of Transitions.

The Six Workshifts

People are going through more transitions—or workshifts, as we call them—more frequently than in the past. Years ago, the relative stability of the workplace meant that people changed jobs infrequently and enjoyed the same basic group of direct reports, bosses and colleagues for years. Today, people are being asked to make huge changes in where and how they work—changes that not only require new skills and knowledge, but psychological adjustments as well.

As an exercise, consider six common workshifts and answer the questions following the list:

- Receiving a promotion to a challenging position
- Being fired
- Getting a new boss
- Being transferred to another country
- Joining a new company with a different culture from a previous employer
- Receiving a stretch assignment

Looking over the list, how many times has each workshift occurred in your career?

How would you rank each workshift in order of difficulty?

What was so challenging about your most difficult workshift? Do you feel it provided any new learnings for you? Was the challenge an adjustment to new people and ways of working?

Do you believe you handled the workshift effectively? With hindsight, what missteps did you make and what would you have done differently?

Most of you have probably gone through at least some of these transitions, likely more than once. It is also likely that you have experienced all sorts of difficulties getting through them, and that you didn't take advantage of the inherent learning in every workshift.

If so, recognize that you're the rule rather than the exception. These transitions are tough. In fact, a study from the Center for Creative Leadership and Lominger, Inc. on learning agility, revealed that only 10% of these thrust into a new situation or transition inquire about it, ask how they might behave differently and then act on recommendations. Approximately 60% of those studied attempted to make some minor adjustments to get through the transition. And 30% could not change their behavior.

So the odds are that you are in the 88% that responds to a significant number of transitions on autopilot. As a result, it is not only difficult to get through the transition successfully, but you don't take any knowledge away from it that can be useful in furthering your career. You never ask yourself "What is going on here?"

When conditioned responses control your actions, you don't ask questions. This is as opposed to when you are aware and adaptable because you've made learning and adaptability part of your mode of operation.

Through this tool called ARTT, you are able to change the self-talk that is going on in your head from negative to positive. It will allow you to navigate successfully through each transition. When you become proficient at it, you are able to reflect and evaluate in real time. You can spot old behavior patterns from similar situations in the past that get you in trouble; you can generate a number of positive alternative actions; you can learn from what you did wrong in the past and from your more productive responses in the present.

Think about what happens to many professionals who receive stretch assignments. They are asked to complete a task for which they feel unqualified or at least ill-prepared. At the first sign of trouble, they revert to old, counterproductive behaviors without thinking. When they run into a time crunch, they cut corners—perhaps they have done this in the past without too many negative consequences. When they need to run a cross-functional team for the first time, they reflexively run it as they have other teams, not acknowledging the differences. They never ask why they are doing these things; they simply do them. At best they make it through the stretch assignment without censure. At worst, they fall short of their objective. In either case, it is a wasted experience because they went through it in a haze, unwilling and unable to step back, think about what they were doing, learn from it and change.

As tough as transitions can be, they are goldmines of learning if you know how to access the learning they contain. As you will see, asking yourself some key questions consistently will help you get at the learning.

Continuous Adapting in Order to Stay Competitive

No doubt, you have heard and read a great deal about the information revolution and knowledge management. There is a reason why everyone is talking and writing about these issues. It may well be that your organization has launched a major knowledge management initiative or invested heavily in information technology. The key is recognizing that every organization values knowledge, whether it is extrinsic or intrinsic. They know that the smarter their people work, the more effective and productive they will be.

ARTT helps professionals improve their work intelligence dramatically. The four step methodology that you will read about in the following chapters is designed to help you pause and ask questions—the how and why of things—as you confront a range of issues. Instead of just moving from point A to point B, you can stop, pause, project impact and adapt.

> You can teach yourself to figure out what you're doing wrong in a given situation, what you're doing right and what additional alternatives you might consider. In this way, each work challenge and transition you go through will serve a purpose beyond the obvious one- you can leverage it to learn and grow. In today's world, learning and growing are absolutely essential for success, no matter what type of job you have or career to which you aspire.

With that point in mind, consider the seven benefits of having *the Skill*:

1. Ability to adapt to and lead change

2. More impactful results and high performance

3. Increased analysis of alternatives

4. Better problem solving

5. Improved relationships

6. More innovative and resourceful thinking

7. Improved self control and peace of mind

To acquire these benefits, you need to learn what is involved in ARTT. As you will discover, it is a process that is accessible to just about everyone and geared for the challenges people face today.

SKILL SAVVY SUMMARY

WHY NOW? AN ERA WHERE *THE SKILL* **COUNTS**

KEY POINTS

- In today's fast paced, complex and information-over-loaded world, adapting to changing conditions is a career necessity.

- Self-awareness facilitates adaptability. It keeps you off of "autopilot", a state of low awareness that prevents you from changing as conditions change.

- On autopilot, you don't question yourself, which inhibits learning as well as adaptability.

CHAPTER 2

Acquiring *the Skill*

"Wake up and smell the coffee."
— Ann Landers: Chicago Tribune, 1955

It would be great if you could go through your work day with instant access to an insightful boss, mentor or coach. Imagine being able to talk with a wise advisor who could point out when you are repeating counterproductive behaviors that have hurt you in the past or suggest new, effective ways for dealing with challenges. It would be wonderful if you could consult with this advisor in real time and talk about how your presentation went or what you did right and wrong in your meeting with an important customer. Perhaps best of all, it would be terrific if this person could formulate a plan

based on your past behaviors that would ensure you would respond more effectively when confronted with both problems
and opportunities.

Unfortunately, most of us don't have 24-hour access to a
personal advisor, let alone a highly insightful one. The good
news is that all of us carry this insightful advisor around inside of us, and it is just a question of learning to tap into this
capability. The essence of *the Skill* is self-awareness combined
with learning and adaptability. With *the Skill* you can deal
with any work situation effectively, no matter what it involves.
Acquiring *the Skill* isn't difficult, as long as you have a model
to guide you. For this reason, we're going to make sure you're
well-versed in ARTT. (See page number 174 for a diagram of
ARTT).It is a process that just about anyone can do with a
little knowledge, a good process and lots of practice. Let's start
with the knowledge component, beginning with defining what
ARTT is - and what it is not.

A Method for Translating Self-Awareness into Action

As this subtitle suggests, ARTT is more than an ad hoc thera-
peutic way of understanding who you are and why you do what
you do. Instead, it is a formal process of self-inquiry, designed to
increase your self-awareness and adaptability to improve performance, promotability and potential. ARTT allows you to learn
continuously from your mistakes, as well as your accomplishments; it spotlights behaviors that make you unsuccessful and
successful in your job; and it helps you transfer what you learn to
new challenges.

The learning that comes from ARTT takes the following
four forms:

- **Specific "pieces" of awareness about yourself.** You will gain a greater awareness of your internal thoughts and feelings. In addition, you will discover the impact your words and actions have externally, on the work situations you encounter every day. When you become aware of what you feel and think and how it guides what you say and do, this integration of internal and external changes how you view your behaviors.

- **A from-to dynamic.** ARTT is not just about figuring out where you want to go toin your career or as a professional. It is about becoming aware of where you are coming from—what you have done in the past and are doing in the present—in order to move to a future goal.

- **Answers to the "why" and "how" questions.** People are so eager to learn what to do in order to achieve greater career success that they ignore the why and how. The ARTT process helps you grasp why and how you do something, and then provides ways for you to adapt what you do based on the why and how. This method of adapting your behaviors is superior to a purely what approach.

- **Alternatives.** This process provides you with options for action rather than forcing you to follow one path. ARTT

is not based on a particular theoretical
construct or bias about what works in
careers. Instead, its guiding principle is
that adaptability is crucial today and will
be even more crucial in the future, and
that having options makes adapting to
circumstance that much easier.

As explained in the Introduction, thousands of people at all
types of organizations have experienced these learnings using
the ARTT method. Starting in Chapter 4, we'll explain how to
use the Awareness, Reflect, Target and Try components of the
four-step ARTT process. Here, though, we want to focus on its
overarching concepts. We want to provide an understanding of
its fundamentals before introducing you to the process steps.

Think about it this way. Let's assume you have the where-
withal to hire the best career coach in the world. You figure
this world-renowned coach will provide you with far greater insight and advice than you can produce on your own. In reality
though, this coach can spend relatively little time with you; he
has other clients and commitments. Therefore, you're on your
own for 39 hours out of 40 each week. Your coach cannot be
there when you're facing a tough work decision or having a difficult conversation with a colleague. You lack the time or opportunity to contact your coach when you're in the middle of
heated exchange with your boss or when you're trying to sell a
prospective customer.

The reality is we live life "on the fly." In other words, what
we learn and what we do with this learning occurs in the moment that it is happening. We're on our own to learn from past
mistakes and apply what we learned to a specific situation. And
that is where ARTT is invaluable.

Here's an analogy that makes this point crystal clear. Let's say you decide to take up tennis and want to learn to play competitively. You need a coach to teach you how to play and train you. If you take a one hour lesson per week, you can learn some fundamental skills over a period of time. But what happens when you play a match? Your coach probably is not there. Even if he is in attendance, he can't do much to help you if you're having one of those matches where you are struggling to get your backhand shot over the net. You must step back, observe yourself in action, reflect on what you're doing wrong and self-correct in the moment based on what you've learned. In a matter of seconds, you become conscious that you are not bending your knees sufficiently and you are raising your racket too high. It is then that you adapt, change your stance and racket position and hit the ball more effectively.

This does not mean there is no need for a coach. It simply means that you must use self-inquiry and apply your learnings to capitalize on the numerous opportunities that occur every single day.

We should also discuss the relationship between ARTT and more traditional skill-building. We are all for developing skills, but that is not the objective of ARTT. Its goal is to help people apply *the Skills* that they already have more effectively, particularly under stressful conditions. Due to increased self-awareness through self-inquiry, they can apply their strengths to navigate challenging situations and improve their performance. In addition, by using ARTT, they give themselves the opportunity to use strengths to build skills.

For example, let's say you have a blow-up with a colleague and you receive feedback from your boss that you're a poor listener and that's what caused the conflict. If you take a communications course or work at trying to be a better listener, you may make some slight improvement in your ability to listen. By using ARTT, however, you would become aware that while you are generally a good listener, you tend to misinterpret what other people say when you're under stress or upset; that this has been a pattern in your career. With this awareness, you can recognize your tendency to become deaf when under stress or when you are angry, and develop a "listening system" to implement in targeted situations.

Before looking at how ARTT puts people in control of their work behaviors, we want to answer a question that clients often ask us: Don't you have to be a therapist or at least receive some training as a coach before you can implement the ARTT process?

Absolutely not! Coaching and ARTT are two very different methods. The latter is a tool of self-inquiry. ARTT is like an operating system for your computer in that once you have it installed, it runs all programs. As such, you really need nothing more than the process to help you ask the right questions and know what to do with the answers. Perhaps more significantly, you've been coaching yourself all your life. Think of all the conversations that run through your head after you have experienced failures or successes in a job. This self-talk is at the heart of ARTT, and it's simply a matter of using this self-talk constructively, rather than destructively. We all have become accustomed to giving ourselves advice after we've messed up an assignment; or we tell ourselves that we should try to replicate a behavior that brought us success with a previous assignment. The question is whether this is good advice. A proven self-inquiry process, with its techniques and tactics, generally produces such advice. To access it, you're simply taking a familiar mode of inquiry to a higher level.

To prove this point, think about whether you've ever been coached in the past or gone to a therapist. Did you agree with the coach's or therapist's conclusions or advice? If you did agree with it, what did you do with the advice? Consider how you applied the suggestions you received at work or in relationships? With hindsight, doesn't it seem you coached yourself in order to put the advice into practice?

Switch Off Autopilot, Switch on Your Awareness

When you use *the Skill*, you combat your natural tendency to operate on autopilot. You may be unfamiliar with this as it applies to behavior, but it's a crucial term for understanding the ARTT approach. Defined, autopilot describes a mode of living or working in which little purposeful or active thinking takes place. It is synonymous with unconscious behavior. You can simulate this state by remembering a time when you drove home from a tough day at the office or back from the airport after a stressful business trip, and during the drive a disjointed tape of the stressful moments earlier in the day replayed in a loop in your mind. All of a sudden, you arrive at your home and have no memory of the drive. You drove home in a kind of daze and can't even remember stopping at lights or making turns down particular streets. In short, you were operating on autopilot.

Autopilot may seem like a benign state, but it is an insidious condition that can diminish work effectiveness and destroy careers. You would think that smart, savvy professionals would avoid autopilot since it's clearly not in their best interest to go through work unaware of what's going on inside of them, yet even some CEOs fall into the autopilot trap. This is a phenomenon that has an illustrative parallel in nature. John Fabre, a French naturalist, conducted an experiment involving processionary caterpillars. As the name implies, these caterpillars blindly follow the one in front of it. In the experiment, Fabre placed a flowerpot filled to the rim with dirt and pine needles, which provides these caterpillars with sustenance. The caterpillars were released next to the flowerpot and traveled in a processionary circle around the flowerpot, and within a short period of time, all the caterpillars dropped dead of starvation, even though food was just six inches away.

They were marching on autopilot, unable to break the unthinking grip of their habitual behaviors even to save themselves.

Many professionals are locked into similar routines. They run meetings the same way they have for years. They interact with customers as they have always interacted with them. They deal with crises in the same manner as they have dealt with crises in the past. As a result, they don't take into consideration if an old approach that may have worked 15 years ago still works. They don't recognize that an ingrained behavior that may seem to help them get things done is actually alienating others and causing more problems than it is solving.

Never underestimate the hold that autopilot has on people's behaviors. It is so powerful because it is so comfortable. It feels familiar so it feels right. More than that, autopilot offers the illusion of being in control. Autopilot usually is switched on so you can deny and avoid harsh realities. If you switch autopilot on, you think you are in control, when all you have done is avoided and denied what is really taking place. When the switch is in the "on" position, you feel like you can simply act without thinking. You don't have to deal with the uncertainty of a new type of behavior or take any risks. On the surface, it feels like you are responding appropriately. As a result, it is difficult to motivate yourself to leave this comfort zone.

The Skill can facilitate your departure from comfortable mediocrity. Please understand that we're not suggesting that you become a completely different person and act in ways that are out of character or that don't take advantage of your proven strengths. We're simply saying that you need to develop a deeper awareness that allows you to operate without autopilot. In this way, you can vary from the routine and try some new and more effective behaviors in given situations. As you will discover, when you become aware of the self-talk going on inside of you, you are much better able to discard the comfortable autopilot state.

Talking to Yourself: What You Say has Value

Self-talk is another concept essential for grasping the ARTT approach. Though we all talk to ourselves (usually it takes the form of a silent interior monologue or dialogue), we are not always aware of this self-talk. Much of this conversation takes place in our sub-conscious, and we may only catch bits and pieces of it. Many times, a specific event triggers self-talk: you are fired from a job and begin a long conversation with yourself about why you were let go, what you might have done differently to prevent it and so on.

> Self-talk can have a positive or negative impact on your career, depending on if it is based in reality. Too often, even the smartest professionals engage in counterproductive self-talk.

They tell themselves they were fired from their last three jobs because their bosses were jerks, rationalizing all the personality conflicts that actually led to their being fired. Because they can't face the fact that they are oversensitive to criticism, their self-talk prevents them from changing their behavior in a way that would help their careers. Similarly, deceptive self-talk may produce low self-esteem, convincing people that they should never apply for a new job or take on a stretch assignment. You may have been fired for reasons that had nothing to do with your performance—you got caught in a 10% across the board staff reduction—but you tell yourself that you were fired because you couldn't cut it. This causes you to apply only for low-level jobs because you don't think you can handle anything more ambitious.

By learning how to tune into your self-talk and root it in reality, you are able to assess situations accurately and choose appropriate actions. Admittedly, it takes a bit of work before you can eliminate the deceptive and overly negative tone of self-talk, but we'll provide some techniques that will provide a clear channel to hear this internal dialogue. You will discover your self-talk can be more instructive than 360 degree feedback. It is reality-based, real time information, and it provides you with a meaningful foundation upon which you can take action.

How People Respond to the Process

As you might imagine, some people are more adept at this process than others. We've had clients who have picked up the process with astonishing speed while others take a bit more time. Some people are good at some aspects of it while they're not so good at others. For instance, Faye is a top executive with a major corporation. She had recently joined the company from a much smaller one, where Faye was a big fish in a small pond. In her new role, she continued to dominate discussions and finish other people's sentences with her own ideas, just like she did in her previous corporation. Faye used to be able to get away with this behavior, in part because she simply had much more experience and expertise than her colleagues. Here though, Faye's behavior prevents others with great expertise and ideas from contributing also created unproductive conflict within her team.

When we began working with her, Faye responded well to the ARTT process and quickly mastered the A (Awareness). She was alert for those moments when she began to dominate meetings and would attempt to take a step back and solicit a diversity of opinions. Unfortunately, Faye was not a quick study when it came to executing based on her awareness. She would only let others talk as long as she agreed with their ideas. As soon as their position diverged from hers, Faye would interrupt and push people in her direction.

It took another month of working with Faye, but she gradually began to see the mistake she was making and how she was subverting her own self-coaching. She became more aware of her tendency to get caught up in the heat of the moment and relapse to autopilot. Faye would become so worked up defending her own position in her mind when someone offered an opposing view that she would try to bully people into her way of thinking. To prevent this from happening, Faye needed an "early warning system" to remind her of this tendency, so she could engage in ARTT. As a remedy, Faye was to bring a hot cup of coffee to each meeting. She was not to voice her own opinion until that coffee had become cold; every warm sip of coffee reminded her to let others speak and interact with each other.

Therefore, recognize that you may struggle a bit with certain aspects of the process, and that you may need an early warning system such as the "hot coffee technique" to help you master a given component in the process.

If you believe in the value of self-inquiry, you will look forward to your self-talk and how it helps you adapt to changing conditions. You will see significant gains in your performance and your career.

Monitoring your attitude before starting the ARTT process is an excellent preliminary step. To get a sense of whether your attitude lends itself to the self-coaching process, place an A (Agree) or D (Disagree) next to each of the following statements:

1. I possess the capacity to change how I manage and relate to others in work situations.

2. Even if my career has not gone in the direction I wanted up to this point, am certain I can do what is necessary to get it back on track.

3. I believe I am working at the highest possible level and cannot do any better than I have already done.

4. I am willing to do whatever it takes to reach my job/career goals.

5. As much as I would like to believe it, I know that I cannot really advance much because of my age, the downsized industry I am in, etc.

6. I tend to beat myself up whenever I make a work mistake and worry that I just do not have what it takes to get ahead.

7. Though I have not received every promotion I wanted or achieved the success I expected, I have great faith in my capacity to achieve my goals.

8. When things are not going my way at work, I cope by withdrawing and waiting until things get better.

The following are the "correct" answers from an attitude perspective. If you had some incorrect answers, the next chapter's focus on how ARTT can help your career may encourage you to adjust your attitude.

Answers

1.	A	5.	D
2.	A	6.	D
3.	D	7.	A
4.	A	8.	D

SKILL SAVVY SUMMARY

ACQUIRING THE SKILL

KEY POINTS

- The Skill is a four-step process of self-inquiry to examine WHAT, HOW, and WHY you do what you do.

- The Skill toolset begins with a mental pause; it gives you the space to question your actions and takes you off of autopilot.

- Ground the self-talk that guides your questions in reality; keep it positive.

- Self-talk can be positive or negative, based on your beliefs and attitudes, so be aware of what they are and how they're impacting your self-talk.

CHAPTER 3

How *The Skill* is Essential to Your Career

"You can't argue with success."
— Anonymous Modern Proverb,
New York Times, 1963

Everyone's career has the potential to go in the ditch, but you possess the capability to prevent this unfortunate occurrence. Today, you cannot depend on others to keep you out of the ditch and help you achieve your career goals. You can't solely depend on your organization, your mentor, your boss or an outside advisor. Years ago, you may have been fortunate to work for an organization that took care of you, that nurtured your talents and that helped you reach your career objectives.

In our current climate, it is difficult to find an organization that treats its people in this manner. Similarly, bosses no
longer have the time to work closely with their people and develop them in ways that boost both their productivity and their
careers. Mentors are few and far between, and those that exist
tend to provide more in terms of emotional support than practical advice—their suggestions, though well-intentioned, often are
not in tune with the current organizational realities and politics.
While excellent outside coaches exist, their ability to help people
navigate their careers is limited. As we have noted, they are not
available at a moment's notice 24/7; they may see their clients
once a week or once a month.

And as our first chapter demonstrated, people need wise
counsel now more than they ever have before. The volatility
within organizations and in the world at large demands that people make a rapidly increasing number of transitions, and most
individuals adapt poorly as they go through these transitions.

So you are on your own to deal with major work changes, shifts
and transitions. But you don't have to be without resources. ARTT
is *the Skill* you need to help you deal with both the problems and the
opportunities that you encounter throughout your career. It can
make you more effective in your job, more marketable and more
capable of handling a broader and more challenging range of assignments. Before examining how this is so, we need to provide you
with an all too familiar cautionary lesson of what happens when you
fly by the seat of your pants and your career goes off course.

Going in the Ditch

For us, this is a better term than the more commonly used "de-
railed" to describe what happens to people's careers at a time of

great transition. The changes literally blow them off their career paths, depositing them in a ditch from which it's difficult to extricate themselves and get back on their desired paths.

People most commonly end up in the ditch because of changing career conditions. They are thrown off by a new boss, an acquisition of their company, a new job and so on. Without the ability to utilize self-talk through these transitions, they end up learning nothing at best and losing their job at worst.

Consider the case of Jim Fisher. He had been with his mid-sized company for 15 years before being promoted to a vice president position and placed in charge of all operations in the region. Shortly after his promotion, Jim's company was acquired and a new CEO was appointed. After three months this CEO announced a new strategy, one that set highly ambitious objectives for both the organization and its senior leaders. The CEO also advocated a change in the way senior leadership operated, recommending new policies and procedures designed to achieve better results.

While Jim agreed with this new strategy in principle, he was not about to change how he ran his region. Jim had a history of delivering excellent results and receiving rewards (promotions, bonuses and other perks) based on his success. He felt that the CEO-mandated changes were fine for other, under-performing senior executives, but not for him. When Jim was confronted by his boss because he was not making the required changes, he offered excuses and continued operating as he had been, on autopilot, assuming that his accomplishments in the past protected him.

They didn't. Eventually Jim was fired because he couldn't adapt to changing conditions. Rather than taking advantage of the opportunities afforded him by a new CEO with a sound, aggressive strategy, he persisted in operating as he always had. ARTT would have made him aware of his self-destructive behaviors. Jim would have realized that his pride and stubbornness were causing him to resist change for resistance's sake—a pattern that had surfaced in his previous interactions with bosses. In addition, Jim could have used the new objectives and operational protocols to learn and grow; he could have acquired the knowledge and skills that would have made him a more marketable candidate for higher-level jobs within his company and elsewhere.

Instead, Jim ended up in a career ditch and looking for a new job.

The Three P's

> The problem, of course, is that you won't be promotable, a solid performer or display high potential if you're residing in a career ditch. ARTT provides you with a way to stay out of the ditch and the tools needed to enhance your 3 P's. To understand how this is so, let's look at each P individually:

Promotability

If you're promotable, you demonstrate political savvy, are highly responsive to your boss, are around and involved with people who matter; you're also ambitious, hard-working and a persuasive communicator. If you're promotable, you have great relationship-building skills—with bosses, peers and direct reports—and don't create collateral damage in order to meet your group's goals. In short, you're someone who is a solid candidate for plum jobs and attractive to headhunters.

ARTT fosters these promotable traits. For instance, it's natural for talented executives and managers to become complacent to rest on their laurels. You may be assigned a project and be tempted to coast. If you're highly aware of how you are acting in a given situation—if you're using the ARTT process—you don't develop the type of bad habits that allow you to be perceived as a little lazy, an inconsistent communicator and arrogant. Even when you are under stress because you're going through some type of transition, your self-awareness prevents you from taking short cuts or allowing relationships to deteriorate. You catch yourself when you're acting in ways that alienate the boss, even when you feel he is getting in the way of accomplishing key tasks. You coach yourself to avoid burning bridges with someone who can play a significant role in your career.

To understand how the ARTT process helps increase your promotability, consider the following two lists of traits:

- Political savvy — Tell people what they want to hear
- Ambitious — Create relationship collateral damage
- Boss responsive — Yes person
- Visible — Self promoter/blames others
- Confident — Arrogant

When you are on autopilot, you often exhibit at least some of the behaviors and attitudes on the right. You do so because you are allowing patterns and problems from your past to affect your actions in the present. Perhaps you grew up in a household with overly critical parents, and perhaps you had unpleasant experiences with an overly critical boss early in your career. Even though your current boss may want to know your opinions, you tell him what he wants to hear because you lack the awareness to correct yourself. As a result, you behave in a way that makes you appear less promotable than someone who speaks his mind and delivers strong insights and ideas without fear of censure.

When you utilize *the Skill*, on the other hand, you project a very different image, one that makes you an attractive candidate for all types of challenging positions. When you operate and function using ARTT, you gain a level of confidence that is palpable. You also develop the political savvy that is only possible when you're keenly aware of the image you are projecting in a variety of situations—you become astute about how to adjust your behaviors to fit different groups and environments.

Performance

If you perform well, you meet or exceed management's expectations in terms of results. This means you're able to get things done that management wants done, and that you are smart about focusing your time on mission critical projects (rather than wasting it on pet projects of less importance). Your ability to execute makes you extraordinarily valuable at a time when results are critical.

The more you use ARTT, the better you perform. Most people are capable of performing at a high level. Unfortunately, most people don't use this capacity to its fullest. That is because they get sidetracked on tangents, diminish their production because of conflicts with others or do any one of a 100 things that harm performance. Most of these individuals are unaware that they are sabotaging their ability to get things done. In any given moment, they are absolutely convinced they must devote all their energy to competing with a colleague for a larger slice of the budget. They don't realize that they are letting all sorts of personal and emotional issues drive their behaviors, and that these behaviors are not in the best interests of the organization or their careers.

ARTT makes people aware that these personal, often subconscious forces are influencing and controlling their actions and hurting their performance. To get a better idea of what this looks like, take a look at the comparisons below:

- Drive   — Workaholic
- Determination   — Obsesses about the issue
- Discipline   — One track; not flexible
- Task oriented   — Relationship/people issues
- Outcomes-based   — Poor process

Again, the traits on the right are indicative of someone who is on autopilot. When you're aware of or reflecting on why you are acting a certain way, you can lapse into workaholism and assume that because you are working around the clock, you are being productive. When you are self-aware using ARTT, however, you realize that your work efforts need to be focused on critical tasks—especially ones aligned with management objectives. In these instances, you pay attention to what you are doing and why, and the result is drive—a clear and committed focus on key responsibilities.

Potential

In essence, this means you have the capability of doing more—of taking on tougher assignments and meeting more challenging objectives. Potential has become a much more important career-maker (or career-breaker), given the need for managers to step up and deal with new and often unfamiliar situations. What's required is for you to use your current skills and knowledge and apply them to solve problems or seize opportunities that you have never encountered before. People who have the potential to accomplish these ambitious objectives and transition into new roles are prized by organizations.

It is difficult to live up to your potential if you are locked into patterns of behavior, demonstrating an inflexible mindset. When you are on autopilot, your responses to new problems are similar to your responses to old problems; the way you try and take advantage of opportunities is the way you took advantage of them in the past. This is okay if you work in a static environment, but it prevents you from progressing beyond a certain level when conditions are constantly changing.

> *The Skill* confers the ability to expand your repertoire. You can turn on a dime, making changes in your approach based on the ARTT process. You're constantly evaluating your actions and attitudes through questions, and this evaluation gives you the information you need to make adjustments if necessary.

In other words, it frees you from being a slave to a singular approach. You can take what you know and use it in new and creative ways, helping you work effectively as major changes occur on your watch.

Again, here is a list of two types of ways of responding to Potential:

- Why and how
- Open to input
- Adjusts on line
- Asks the right questions
- Obtains results under changing conditions and with stretch assignments

— What (to do)
— Myopic focus
— Follows a prescribed path
— Knows the answers

— Obtains results only under narrow conditions

Many people come into organizations as high potentials, yet they never achieve their potential because of their rigid, narrow and unquestioning approach. If you compare the two lists, you'll notice that the one on the left is characterized by tremendous flexibility and openness. ARTT fosters these two qualities, allowing people to realize their potential in even the most challenging of situations.

The True Predictor of Success

It used to be thought that career success was based on current skill sets or past performance. While it obviously is important to develop key skills and have a good track record, these factors are no longer the major reasons people succeed or fail. That's because things change. They change often and they change in major ways.

You may have spent 20 years with a company, climbed the ladder steadily to an executive position and acquired the compe-

tencies the job specs say are required to obtain a senior leadership position. You have no black marks on your record, no gaps
between what you know and what knowledge is required for key
positions.

Despite all this, your career at a given company can be over
in a heartbeat. All it takes is a merger or acquisition; a new
CEO comes in and requires different skills for his top people and
doesn't really care about your track record under another CEO.
Or it may be that increasing global competition makes it man-
datory for leaders in your field to possess skills and experiences
you lack. Or it may be that a new technology transforms your
business, and your knowledge and skills are no longer as valuable
as they once were.

ARTT can help you survive and thrive in a changing world,
allowing you to become a highly adaptable professional. You
need to be able to learn, grow and change your approach with
great speed. You can't be an adaptable professional if you are
stuck on autopilot. Your ability to learn and apply these learnings will help you adapt with increasing facility. As it helps
you acquire or enhance the 3 P's, it also helps you increase your
flexibility.

It doesn't happen overnight. It demands that you practice
creating Awareness, using Reflection, Targeting changes you
can make and Trying to make these changes consistently.

To thrive in this competitive business environment, *the Skill*
must become part of your professional DNA, and to help you take
the first step in that direction, let's focus on the A in ARTT.

SKILL SAVVY SUMMARY

HOW THE SKILL IS ESSENTIAL TO YOUR CAREER

KEY POINTS

- Monitor the constantly changing conditions in your work environment. Failure to be aware of these changes and how they impact you can diminish your work performance and career options.

- The four-step ARTT process, the toolset to acquire the Skill, will get you off of autopilot. Being off of autopilot will keep you from going in the ditch and most likely from derailing your career.

- Adaptability, versatility and the ability to learn from your experiences help you perform at your highest potential and achieve future success. You need to be motivated to acquire them.

- The ARTT method facilitates acquisition of key capabilities. The more proficient you become at using ARTT, the more you'll develop *the Skill*.

CHAPTER 4

Aware: What Really Happened and What Was My Role?

"I fear all we have done is to awaken a sleeping giant
and fill him with a terrible resolve."

— Isoroku Yamamoto,
Japanese Admiral, 1942

This first step in the ARTT process can be a giant one for
many professionals. Like many people, you may have spent most
of your time doing, rather than thinking about what you have
done. This is understandable given the stretch projects and ambitious objectives you have probably encountered. Without focusing on the task at hand, you could not operate efficiently. Yet

as we alluded to earlier, the autopilot mentality of "doing" can land you in a career ditch.

Therefore, this first step is designed to heighten **your** awareness of your reactions in common business situations and how **your** thoughts, feelings and behaviors impact situations.

Because so many people operate on autopilot and lack awareness, their behaviors and choices are driven by unconscious fear and unresolved painful memories. As they become more aware, they see how they were actors in given situations and played a particular role. The more aware they become of their role, the easier it is to take charge of it. Ultimately, they can see and alter their role and positively impact outcomes.

You can raise your awareness by asking yourself key questions. For instance, after a particular event takes place at work, ask yourself: "What happened?" or "What is working, what is going well and what isn't?" or "What impact is my behavior having on this situation, positively or negatively?" Upon asking and processing the "what" questions, you'll immediately raise your awareness quickly and substantially.

To help you understand how to ask these types of questions and make use of the answers, we need to define what awareness is from a practical standpoint.

Total Versus Partial Awareness

Most people suffer from partial self-awareness without realizing it. They believe that because they have a good sense of their own identity, they are able to function at peak effectiveness in work situations. They are certain they know their strengths and weaknesses, and they often are supremely confident in their ability to make quick decisions and solve problems "instantly."

In reality, however, they are only aware of what is going on inside of their own heads. They may think they know themselves well because they understand their most obvious tendencies and skills, but they never step back and question how their behaviors affect others. They don't think about their behaviors holistically; they don't see how their strengths and weaknesses impact different types of situations and individuals. Their very confidence causes them to react, rather than reflect, and they end up on autopilot.

> True awareness, then, is the ability to be conscious of what is going on inside of you and outside of you, and how who you are and a given situation impact each other.

On the surface, Bob seemed to possess good self-awareness. A vice president of marketing at a large corporation, Bob had been with his company for ten years and had done well. If you were to ask him what his strengths and weaknesses were, he could go through the list without hesitation. He has always been proud of his ability to delegate jobs that are outside of his skill areas and has flourished by playing to his strengths—he is great at coming up with innovative ideas that inspire and direct the company's advertising, sale promotion and public relations efforts.

Ten years after Bob first joined the company, a new CEO was appointed, and he immediately made it clear that he was going to emphasize team play, new systems and improved customer relationships. Instead of thinking about these new requirements in terms of specific situations and his own way of operating, Bob decided to "just be myself." At some level, he convinced himself that if he kept on doing what made him successful in the past, he wouldn't really have to deal with the new CEO's requirements.

After a few months, however, the CEO asked Bob to report on his progress in the three new strategic areas. Bob told him he was making good progress without being specific. Later, when Bob had to make a detailed presentation to the CEO and other senior executives, it became clear that he only responded in token ways to the new initiatives. A week later, the CEO suggested in the strongest possible terms that Bob was not meeting expectations; that he was the only vice president in the organization that had been dragging his feet and that it was creating disconnects within Bob's department as well as with other functions. After the conversation, Bob confided in a colleague that the CEO "doesn't understand our company – it's not like his previous job" and that he would soon become tired of trying to force people like Bob to conform to his misconceived strategy.

The CEO didn't become tired, and Bob was fired. Bob was on autopilot. Unknowingly, he was filtering out key pieces of information about himself and the new situation at his company. Though his boss was clearly communicating that Bob needed to improve in three areas, Bob refused to acknowledge that he had to change anything about the way he led or managed. It is not that Bob was out of touch with who he was in a psychological sense. It was that his awareness started and ended with his own identity.

Fully aware people use self-inquiry to understand how their actions or inaction impact a given situation or other individuals. They engage in self-questioning that raises their consciousness level, providing them with the insight to understand their impact. These questions are critical, and Bob didn't ask them of himself. He didn't ask: What are the CEO's expectations of me; what did I do or not do that caused me to get fired? What does this mean to my career?

Asking these questions fosters a deep awareness. Asking none

of these questions results in a kind of myopia where people see
only what they want to see. To help you understand the practical differences between being aware and unaware, consider the
following chart:

Aware	Unaware
• Observes their impact on situations or others	• Focuses on their agenda or task at hand
• Knows strengths and weaknesses	• Fails to understand their limits; overconfident
• Asks questions and seeks understanding	• Has quick answers
• Is candid and seeks feedback	• Avoids discussions about themselves
• Learns from mistakes	• Blames others
• Empathizes (puts themselves in others' shoes)	• Sees things only from their perspective
• Is open to criticism	• Is defensive

Obviously, these two columns represent opposite ends of
an awareness continuum. Most people are not purely aware or
purely unaware, but exist somewhere in between. The goal,
though, is to move closer to the Aware ideal. This can be done
in a number of ways, but let's look at one awareness-building
technique that we've found to be highly effective.

Instant Replay

Self-awareness comes in two forms. First, you can go through a given situation and then afterwards debrief yourself on what took place. Second, you can "hit pause" in the middle of the situation, evaluating your thoughts and feelings in real time. Clearly, the second approach is more challenging, so let's look at how to create after-the-fact awareness.

When you debrief yourself, you should focus on the following questions relative to the event/situation that just occurred:

- What were you thinking?
- What were you feeling?
- What you were saying?
- What you were doing?

The first two questions involve internal responses, the second two questions relate to external behaviors. Both are critical, but when you first attempt to access information relating to them, you may feel a little uncomfortable trying to recreate what may have been a difficult situation. You may also find it difficult to know how to go about it. This type of ability is similar to the instant replay process in NFL football games.

Coaches in the NFL use the technology's ability to pause, identify and evaluate previous plays. For example, in 2005, Mike Tomlin was named as the defensive coordinator of the Minnesota Vikings, and in one year he took the defensive squad from one of the lowest rankings in the league to the top defense against the run in 2006. Tomlin had every defensive player watch a tape of the previous week's game and grade himself on his execution on each play.

In this way, Tomlin was teaching his players how to become more aware and self-coach. The following year, Tomlin was named head coach of the Pittsburgh Steelers, where he will no doubt use this same technique and achieve similarly stellar results.

Everyone is going to implement this instant replay in his or her own way, but the key is to engage in a conversation with yourself about what took place. As soon as you do this, you increase your self-awareness. Earlier, we noted four general questions designed to guide your debriefing after a particular event. Here are three more specific questions that will help you accomplish the same goal:

- What was really going on (what just took place, both the specific words and behaviors of those involved and the results/ possible consequences; what is a bottom line summary of this particular event)?

- What was my role in this situation (what part did you play; what were you responsible for; were you a facilitator, roadblock, catalyst, non-participant)?

- What was the impact of your behavior (how did others experience you; what were the results for others based on what you said or did)?

Think about that first question for a moment. Let us say you just came from a meeting in which you discussed cost overrun solutions with your team, and one member of your team, Dianne, dominated the discussion with her ideas. Dianne is talented, but overbearing, and you have put up with her because she has been a strong contributor in the past. Now, though, as you replay the meeting and observe your own performance, you realize that because you allowed Dianne to dominate, no one else really had a chance to say much of consequence. "Did I allow Dianne to stifle everyone else's ideas?" you ask yourself. This question fosters awareness that leads to action. If you don't ask the question, your awareness level is low and you don't do anything about a potentially negative situation. When you think about your role in the meeting, you learn that you were a non-participant, at least in the larger sense of that word. While you may have run the meeting, you let Dianne run over you. And your behavior communicated to everyone that you are an easily manipulated manager.

Instant replay creates this type of self-awareness. Your replay session may not be as "instant" as this example and it may require some practice using different types of probing questions until you "get" what is really going on. Still, we want to emphasize here that you possess an instant replay capability, and that it is a great tool for helping yourself become more self-aware.

All this brings up the question of what "blocks" this self-awareness during the typical work day? If it is that easy, why are most people stuck on autopilot and not aware? Is it that we are just not paying attention? Or is the cause something deeper?

Pain Lumps: What Hides Behind Our Hurt

There's a reason the manager in our previous example failed to stop Dianne from acting in a way that was clearly counterproductive. Most of us are reluctant to get in touch with childhood fears and painful memories from our past. When we begin asking ourselves questions like, "Why did I allow Dianne to act that way in the meeting?"we uncover these fears. This manager may have had a parent who terrorized him as a child or it may have been a different type of hurtful experience, but whatever it was, it's not something he wants to revisit as an adult.

Unfortunately, people who don't "process" this fear and pain from their past will have a more difficult time getting off of autopilot and becoming more aware. They spend all their energy managing their emotions and keeping this hurtful past hidden from themselves. We refer to this negative experience as a "Pain Lump." A "Pain Lump" can be easily described as a negative stored memory that you are not aware you have.

Scott, for instance, has experienced a great deal of emotional trauma in his life, including an unhappy childhood and the death of his father at a relatively young age. Everyone experiences difficult events such as these. Scott, though, has refused to understand how these events impacted him and his behavior. He doesn't think or talk about them except in the most superficial ways. As a result, the Pain Lump forms and resides in his subconscious memory. That lump is always there and obscuring the reasons behind his behavior. Scott came across in work settings as a cold, un-empathetic boss. More than one performance review had raised this issue, but Scott rationalized it away; he told himself that the fault resided with his direct reports rather than him; that they wanted to be pampered and his role was to "toughen them up."

For years, Scott had been stuck in a middle management position despite his strong strategic skills and ability to get things done on time and with great results. Scott had always assumed that politics prevented him from moving to a senior level job. He had told his wife that he wasn't the sort of person who was good at playing games or working a room.

When Scott started discussing his situation with a close friend, he began to realize that there was another explanation. Through a number of coffees and conversations, the friend encouraged Scott to think about his work behaviors in a broader context. The friend asked Scott if anyone at work reminded him of a parent or relative, and Scott mentioned that his boss's boss was highly emotional, and unpredictable just like both of his parents. This led Scott to recall how difficult it was growing up as the only child of a mother and father who were outsized personalities—his father had a quick temper, but he also possessed a boisterous sense of humor. His mother could be moved to tears when she saw a dead deer on the side of the road, but she was also a screamer when things didn't go her way. Overwhelmed by these volatile parents, Scott responded by keeping his feelings to himself, favoring logic over emotion.

When Scott realized that his Pain Lump had its origins in being the son of highly emotive parents, he gained a greater understanding of why he behaved as he did in organizational settings. This understanding eventually helped him become acutely aware of when he was acting like a "cold fish."

Awareness Alert: Signs That You are Hiding Your Pain

We naturally hide our pain. Like Scott, we are clever about pretending everything is fine and that we are in complete control of our behaviors. Nine out of ten people with huge Pain Lumps would tell you that nothing in their past is governing their attitudes or actions in the present. They would insist that they are highly aware of their situations at work.

Because of this denial reflex, it is useful to know the six signs of "unawareness," as well as the overarching emotion that indicates a Pain Lump is doing damage. Let's start with the six signs:

1. **Stress sensitivity.** Yes, people can be under stress for perfectly legitimate reasons related to deadlines, stretch assignments and so on. Nonetheless, this is a sign that a painful experience from the past is being ignored when the level of stress is out of proportion to the circumstance. When people have difficulty coping with a situation that isn't particularly problematic or overwhelming, then it's a sign of a pain lump.

2. **Vague worry.** In other words, you feel a constant sense of worry or unease, but you can't name the cause. The reason you can't pinpoint the cause is because it's buried in the past.

3. **Hair-trigger anger.** While everyone gets angry, this sign relates to anger that seems to come out of nowhere. One moment you're having a normal conversation, the next you're furious. What happened is that someone has touched a nerve, only it's a nerve that has nothing to do with work.

4. **Deep discouragement.** You fail to receive an assignment or your project failed to receive a green light. Disappointment is natural in these situations, but you feel more discouraged than you've been in years.

5. **Adolescent self-consciousness.** You frequently feel awkward and embarrassed. You walk around thinking people are talking about you behind your back and laughing at you.

6. **Shockingly impulsive.** This goes beyond being occasionally spontaneous. It may manifest itself as rash decisions or a willingness to take unnecessary risks. Instead of doing due diligence or analyzing before acting, you get carried away and make choices without much or any thought.

The Fear Factor: Recognize It Rather than Run from It

Finally, there is fear. Fear is the product of having a Pain Lump. Think of it this way: a toddler almost drowns, but as a teenager, he has little or no conscious memory of this awful event. Yet when he and his friends go to the beach, he is absolutely terrified of going in the water over his head. That Pain Lump serves as a block—a block of which he is unaware. All he feels is fear.

At work, this fear can be a sign of something blocking you. Perhaps you refuse to apply for any jobs above a certain level, even though you are qualified for them. Maybe you know your boss is pursing an ill-fated strategy but you are reluctant to confront him. Your fear prevents you from taking action, to the detriment of your job performance and career aspirations.

At the same time, that fear is like a dark, creepy cave. As much as you're scared of the dark, you are even more frightened of flicking on a light and seeing your demons.

We'll talk later about how to confront these demons. For now though, pay attention to the six signs and your sense of fear. They are tipping you off that you are not particularly aware of your behaviors and how they are impacting others.

Seeing Yourself on the Stage

Awareness is really about the ability to step back and observe yourself. If you think of your work life as a play, then you want to be more than an actor in it—an actor who simply recites rehearsed lines and lacks the ability to improvise. You want to be both actor and director, and in the latter role, take a step back, observe the action and make changes to improve the play.

Imagine yourself in a critical encounter at work—you are making a presentation to senior executives or attempting to close a deal with your largest customer. If you're just an actor, all you can do is recite and react. Your options are limited. If you're both director and actor, however, you can "watch" yourself interacting with the senior executives or the customer. You can evaluate your performance in the moment, determine how others are experiencing you and change it on the fly if necessary.

Of course, this description represents the highest state of awareness. Most people need to start out using the instant replay technique and gain awareness after the presentation is concluded. With practice, though, you can achieve the awareness of an actor and a director of the performance.

Make a consistent effort to become more aware. Ask yourself the questions contained in this chapter, not just once or every so often, but all the time. In this way, you'll take yourself off autopilot. A sure sign that you're no longer relying on autopilot is your ability to answer the "what" questions. When others (a coach, a boss, a friend) ask you what happened when you reacted as you did during a meeting, you have a deep sense of awareness. You don't become defensive or offer rationalizations. Instead, you recognize that the pain in your past is impacting your present actions. You also know your alternatives to a given action and why you chose the specific course you took.

By practicing and perfecting being Aware, you raise your consciousness to the point that you are ready to Reflect - the next step in the ARTT process.

**AWARE: WHAT REALLY HAPPEND AND
WHAT WAS MY ROLE?**

KEY POINTS

- True awareness is not only what is going on around you, but just as important, what is going on inside of you.

- Ask yourself four questions regularly to become more aware: What was I thinking; what was I feeling; what was I saying; what was I doing?

- As you begin to ask questions, acknowledge that you are the only one who can change your behavior.

- As you become more aware, you may surface memories that are painful or create anxiety. Focus on managing the pain and anxiety rather than allowing it to distract you from dealing with the situation at hand.

CHAPTER 5

Reflect: Why Did I Do It? What Happened as a Consequence?

"We had the experience but missed the meaning."
— T. S. Eliot: Four Quartets,
Dry Salvages, 1941

After heightened awareness has curtailed your reliance on autopilot, reflection gives you the freedom to delve deeper into understanding "why" you do what you do. It allows you to discover the significance of a situation or an event, and in that significance you can find the key to making behavioral changes—changes that may have a huge impact on your effectiveness and career trajectory.

Think of the Awareness step as helping you grasp "what" is going on inside and outside of you, and the Reflect step as "why" it is going on.

It is not enough to switch off autopilot and be conscious of your actions and how they are affecting others. As important as this is, it still leaves you operating on a surface level. You need to dig deeper in order to learn from your experiences and move toward mastery of *the Skill*.

A Coachable Moment

When you reflect, you have the chance to learn from your experience and transfer that learning to a similar situation in the future. Reflection essentially captures the learning that takes place in a given moment, rather than allowing it to vanish.

Typically, we don't reflect on our experiences therefore we don't learn from them. Too often, we get caught up in all sorts of side issues and don't concentrate on why we behaved or didn't behave a certain way and why it did or didn't work. As a result, we're likely to repeat our unproductive behaviors.

When you start asking yourself "why" questions, however, you create a coachable moment. We realize that coaching may have some negative connotations, but we're using the term to refer to discovering significance and seeking learned principles. During their formative years, children open up to and begin to navigate the world around them by asking "why"questions. These questions foster learning. Similarly, when we ask "why"questions as adults, they help us make sense of our situations and behavior. Coaching that allows us to learn and grow is only possible when we lower our defenses and allow critical knowledge to penetrate. The small epiphanies that children come to when they ask their "why" questions are similar to the small epiphanies that arrive when adults question themselves.

Recognize, though, that many of us resist these epiphanies. More precisely, we fall into a pattern where we rush to judgment. This means that we are quick to blame another person for a conflict or problem. Rather than accept emotional responsibility for the situation, we put the emotion on someone else. As a result, self-exploration doesn't take place. We judge someone else, and so we lack the impetus to reflect and consider why we acted as we did.

For instance, imagine making a big presentation with your team to a prospective customer. During the presentation, the customer asks you a question that suggests he's skeptical of your ability to deliver on a service promise. You respond with a bit more heat than you intended, feeling your integrity has been challenged. When this prospect persists in questioning your service capabilities, you allow others to respond and are unusually quiet for the rest of the presentation. When you hear the next day that the prospect chose to go with a competitor, you're furious and rationalize the loss of the prospect, saying that he was a "jerk" and that having them as a customer would have made life "a living hell."

This rush to judgment prevents any sort of meaningful reflection from taking place. By doing so, you subconsciously placed the emotional burden on the other person, and you're free to avoid thinking about why you were so defensive and angry.

When to Reflect: Options and Results

Reflection can take place in the moment or after the fact. Sometimes, the ARTT process can be difficult to access during intense situations. You're operating on autopilot, even when you've vowed to be more aware during these times. As a result, you can't really reflect on what happened until later when you've achieved some distance from the event. You may require a quiet place, both literally and figuratively, to reflect on your experience.

In-the-moment reflection, though, should be the goal. The quicker you can reflect on a situation and make sense of what happened, the more likely you'll gain a true and deep understanding. We know that in-the-moment reflection can be a challenge, especially as you are just starting to use the ARTT process. Even after you become ARTT-adept, however, your ability to reflect in real time can be situational. For instance, if you're involved in an emotionally intense argument with your boss, you may have difficulty stepping away from your anger to think about what took place objectively. You may need to wait an hour or two before you can reflect.

Similarly, some situations are so complex that it's difficult to sort out everything in the moment. You require more information before you can reflect on your own behavior in a meaningful context. You might need to hear from others who were in attendance and request their feedback. You might need to do some research.

In the majority of instances though, ARTT veterans learn to reflect in the moment. They process what is taking place while it is happening and make sense of it. They have trained themselves to ask the following questions almost simultaneous to a given situation:

- Why am I doing x?

- Why did I act the way I did?

- Why do I feel this way?

- Why should I do something differently?

- Why should I not do something else differently?

If you are able to reflect on these questions in the moment, you can make mid-course corrections even if you're engaging in a heated debate or delivering a scripted presentation. You can veer away from your planned or routine approach and find a better solution. Even if you don't find a better solution, your reflection facilitates learning because you are providing yourself with insightful, real time feedback about what you say and do.

Initially, this approach may seem difficult to pull off. After all, how do you carry on business while also carrying on an internal dialogue? The secret is practice, making the questions listed above a reflex, rather than something you have to labor to use. When you frequently reflect about what you are feeling and thinking, you provide yourself with a feedback loop that helps you edit your behaviors. If you say something that has a negative effect, you know it almost immediately and now take steps to correct yourself. Instead of waking up in the middle of the night and agonizing that your decision was wrong-headed, you can grasp that fact seconds after you make the decision and reverse it before it does you or your organization any harm.

A Few Words About Learning

Reflection "crystallizes" the understanding you gain about yourself into learning nuggets. In other words, reflection offers more than one-time learning. As this book's introduction explained, everyone has an input jack and an output jack. Being aware and reflecting allows you to take in knowledge and learning through the input jack. When you reflect, you gain understanding that is transferable, specific and clear. These nuggets essentially are principles that can guide your future actions.

If, for instance, your reflection suggested you became indecisive when confronted with a stressful situation involving two feuding reports, then rather than make a decision and resolve the conflict you allowed the situation to simmer, you may uncover the following learning principle: I need to be aware of my tendency to be indecisive in stressful situations and fight through my indecisiveness in order to resolve matters effectively.

Or, to put in more succinctly, "Be decisive under stress." This nugget can be useful in all sorts of work situations.

Possessing a few core learning principles reduces your ambiguous feelings. Too often, people lack anything to guide their future behaviors. As a result, they simply knee-jerk react rather than calculate a response and form a learning base. Learning principles help reduce the anxiety, stress and fear that come with a variety of work situations. With these principles, however, you won't become enmeshed in the emotion of a situation. Rather than getting caught up in your own anger or fear, you focus on what you've learned about how to deal effectively (and how not deal ineffectively) with a particular person, decision or event.

The Key: Turning Reflection into Action

Ryan is a mid-level marketing executive with a large corporation, and in a meeting with senior management, he is asked a question about finances. He automatically responds that he has taken care of this financial issue, but it is soon revealed that he hasn't. Ryan assumed one of his direct reports had addressed the issue of securing approval for a non-budgeted expense, but Ryan had never followed up after he requested the direct report take care of it. As a result, the senior-level executive chews him out for dropping the ball.

After the meeting and for the next week or two, Ryan is wrapped up in his emotional responses to his error. He argues with himself for not following up with his direct report; he chastises his direct report for failing to secure the necessary approval. As a result, Ryan not only doesn't learn anything from this experience, but he is so distraught that it renders him less effective, since his concentration isn't what it should be. In fact, Ryan has an unpleasant confrontation with his boss who was also in the senior management meeting, and Ryan accuses him of "not backing me up."

Finally, one night when he can't sleep, Ryan begins questioning himself about what took place in the meeting and why he behaved the way he did. It occurs to him that he made a mistake by telling management that the financial issue was resolved when he wasn't sure if it had been. As he reflects on the problems his actions have caused him and the organization, he recognizes that the best thing would have been to understand why he had acted the way he did, and accept and own up to his actions.

From the time Ryan was little, he had always projected great confidence and knowledge and would "fake it," rather than admit he didn't know something. This attitude is not uncommon for business executives. Many managers are all action and little reflection. They focus on getting things done and can't admit that they don't know something—they can't admit it to themselves or too thers. If Ryan would have mastered the Reflecting step of *the Skill*, he would have understood his behavior and the patterns from childhood. ARTT would have crystallized the following learning principle: "Check your facts." Too often, Ryan bluffed his way through situations, and this approach was no longer working, especially as he moved up in the organization and took on more responsibility.

"Check the facts" became a principle Ryan grew to rely on, and it helped him earn a reputation for accuracy and accountability, eventually leading to a promotion.

As you can see, Ryan's reflection process was informal. He didn't have the benefit of the ARTT process or specific tools to facilitate that process. Nonetheless, he came to a point in his job and in his career when he was prompted to reflect on his management style. It became the turning point in his career, since that reflection helped him address a serious weakness that was holding him back. Imagine, if Ryan would have been a veteran of ARTT and was using it in-the-moment – this situation would have never have happened.

Techniques to Facilitate Reflection

Unlike Ryan, you don't have to rely only on your instinct to foster reflection and learning.

For instance, it might help you crystallize your learning into nuggets if you write down a three to six word phrase that captures the principle you want to follow. Ryan's was "check the facts." Perhaps yours is "look before you leap," or "count to 10 before speaking." Having the principle firmly embedded in your head as a pithy phrase will help you use it the next time it is needed.

Another technique involves asking the right questions. Earlier, we provided you with four questions that catalyze reflection. Now, we want to make these questions a bit more specific. Remember, you don't have to ask these questions verbatim—they are provided to give you a direction and guidance for your self questioning:

1. What happened?

   Why did this happen?

   Why is this significant?

2. What was my role?

   Why did I behave the way I did?

   Why did others react the way they did?

3. What was the impact on my behavior?

   Why is this consequence significant?

   Why are these consequences important to me, to my team, to other individuals?

Reflection functions best when it operates on both levels – internal and external, yielding a learning principle that you can carry around in your head and transfer to applicable situations in the future. To carry it around effectively, you should try to "encapsulate" it.

This means boiling down your learning into a simple, easy to remember bit of understanding—you'll recall our earlier advice to turn it into a simple phrase like Ryan's, "check the facts."

To help yourself create and encapsulate this learning phrase, ask yourself the following question:

If I were to do this again or I could do it over, what would I do differently to achieve a better outcome?

You must ask this question of yourself more than once. In fact, reflection like awareness takes practice. You should make an effort to use this self-inquiry step regularly, and by using it often, it will become second nature. Don't limit your reflection to one sleepless night a year. Even though it worked for Ryan, it generally takes a much more consistent approach for reflection to yield the results people want. In addition, don't make the mistake of limiting reflection to Big Events—you reflect when you fail to get a much-desired promotion, for instance. Reflect after small work events as well as big ones. The more you do it, the more you'll get out of it.

It will also prepare you to Target the best situations where you can apply what you've learned from Reflection.

SKILL SAVVY SUMMARY

REFLECT: WHY DID I DO IT?
WHAT HAPPENED AS A CONSEQUENCE?

KEY POINTS

- Many people fail to learn from their experiences and adjust their behaviors. By learning and applying *the Skill*, you greatly enhance your learning capacity.

- You can apply what you learn in the moment to make mid-course corrections or later after you process your questions and thoughts.

- Reflection extracts meaning from your experiences. By capturing the key learning from your reflection, you can transfer it to new situations.

- Transfer the knowledge you gained from your reflection into future situations by asking yourself: "If I could do this again, what would I do differently?"

CHAPTER 6

Target: Set Up an Opportunity to use What You Learned

"You say you got a real solution well,
you know we'd all love to see the plan."

— The Beatles, Revolution, (1968)

Based on the insights gained from Awareness and Reflection, people are prepared to set a specific goal or target in order to begin behavioral change. Targeting is a crucial step in the ARTT process since, without it, you may simply "resolve" to be a better listener or a more assertive leader but never make it happen. These resolutions, though well meaning, often remain as just nice thoughts and don't result in positive behavioral changes.

On the other hand, locking on to a specific target makes your resolutions actionable. It gives you a way to apply what you've learned in a real business situation. By targeting you can prepare for that moment when you can take positive action which can lead to change. Remember, *the Skill* is not just about what goes on inside of you, but about applying that internal learning to external situations.

Targeting is about setting up a "how would I do it differently?" goal, applying the learning that came out of your reflection. This may sound like a no-brainer, but people often make the mistake of creating targets that are so vague and general, they become too easy to hit, or too difficult.

Therefore, to help you target effectively, we'd like to share three key principles.

Aiming For a Target Where You Can Hit the Mark

Let's say the reflect step of the ARTT process revealed that you tend to become invisible under pressure, that you tighten up and fail to speak in key meetings or when there's a lot on the line. As a result, you vow to change and target "high-pressure" meetings as opportunities to be more assertive.

The odds are that you won't hit this target. It is too vague and uncertain to catalyze productive behaviors. Is a high-pressure meeting one with a direct report who is unhappy with his job assignment and vows to leave unless he's given more responsibility? Is a high-pressure meeting one where there's a looming deadline? Does such a meeting involve your boss; your boss's boss; a customer or prospect? For you, is the highest pressure meeting one where you're responsible for making a pitch or a presentation? Is it a meeting attended by a lot of people or one where there are a few key decision-makers?

Without a specific target, you may find it difficult to know when to apply your reflection-based learning. You may apply it in a situation that involves only moderate pressure. Or you may rationalize not doing anything differently in any of the meetings because you don't deem them high pressure enough.

Therefore, factor in the following three principles as you figure out your target:

1. Set specific and sufficiently challenging goals.

One of the most common mistakes people make is setting the bar too low. Perhaps 80% of the people who work through ARTT initially make this mistake, usually because they want to ensure that they achieve their goals. Doing so, however, is less important than creating a challenging degree of difficulty. You want to stretch to reach your target. Setting your sights high forces you to change your behavior in a significant and noticeable way. If you set the target too low, the change doesn't have much impact. As the old saying goes, no pain, no gain. Of course, you also don't want to create impossible-to-achieve objectives. It is unrealistic to think that you can go from being a shy non-participant in meetings, for instance, to a charismatic star overnight.

Even more important, create a highly specific target. A non-specific target goal might be something along the lines of, "I'm going to be a better listener." A specific goal would be, "I have a meeting with my boss next Friday at 2:00 p.m., and I am going to be a better listener by maintaining eye contact and by summarizing and commenting on the main points he makes."

To set up a specific target, delineate a situation and actions you intend to take in that situation. Look at your calendar and find an event in which you can use new, desired targeted behaviors—specify what those behaviors will be and with whom you will exhibit them.

2. Visualize the target situation as a "from-to" scenario.

Don't simply think of what you're going to do and when. Instead, create a picture in your mind of what you intend to happen, visualizing where you're coming from and where you are going to. In other words, think of how you acted on autopilot when you were in similar situations in the past. Then envision how you will act with the benefit of greater awareness and reflection.

You probably won't be able to replicate your visualized scenario perfectly; situations often have a few surprises in store for everyone. But if you hold your desired behaviors in your mind, you'll have a better chance of saying and doing the things that you visualized. This is best accomplished when you conduct a mental rehearsal of how you will behave when you are in the meeting.

3. Believe your target is something important you can achieve.

If you think about your target as minor or secondary, it will be much tougher to achieve. If you doubt that you're capable of acting in the way that you envisioned, it will be a self-fulfilling prophecy. Therefore, talk to yourself about how this target is your top priority, and how you have the strength to achieve it.

Be positive and committed. Maintain your focus on reaching this objective, and regularly think about its importance in your life. As the target approaches, you'll be prepared for the situation and the new attitude and actions that it requires.

Finding the Right Situation to Target

A common concern of people going through ARTT is how to find the right situation to target. Many times, they have scores of upcoming meetings, presentations and events that might make good targets to test new behaviors. How do they find the best one?

This question really has two answers. The easiest answer is to look for a "follow-up" situation to one that has caused you problems in the past. For instance, if you get into a fight with your boss whenever you meet to talk about a top priority project, you can target the next project meeting. Or if you're having problems with a major customer, you can target your next encounter with that customer. Or if you find yourself being too dominant and stifling other people's ideas during brainstorming sessions, the next session is the perfect target.

It's possible, though, that no natural sequel will present it-

self. Through Awareness and Reflection you may have identified counterproductive attitudes and actions that emerge in a
variety of situations. As a result, you have too many options to
choose from without being certain which is the best one. It's also
possible that you've joined a new organization recently and don't
have sufficient history with people and schedules in the company
to target a follow-up scenario.

   If you're uncertain how to target a situation, try the following exercise:

   *List four or five work experiences from the past few months that
   you feel did not go well; the experiences caused you discomfort or made
   you fearful. Write a short summary of each experience. Now review
   your written descriptions searching for a common theme. Maybe you've
   described encounters with superiors who made you uncomfortable. The
   theme here is obvious—interactions with people or figures of authority
   that have more power and influence than you. Perhaps you've listed situations where you've had to sell—a prospect on giving you his business,
   a boss on giving you a promotion—and you've felt great unease. Again,
   the theme of selling situations is obvious. If you list a series of seemingly
   different situations—a meeting with a direct report requesting additional
   money for a project, a conversation with your IT person requesting you
   change your software protocols—you need to search beneath the surface of
   events for a theme. Why do these different events all make you fearful?
   It could be that at each event, you're being asked to make a tough decision. With that theme in mind, you should target situations where you're
   asked to make difficult decisions.*

   As you search for your theme, keep in mind that you want
to create the from-to targets we discussed previously. In other
words, you want to identify situations where you'll have ample
opportunity to move away from your old behaviors and try new,
more productive ones. The key test of whether you have set an

appropriate target or not is seeing if, when you think about the target, you feel uncomfortable. This means you are out of your comfort zone, where most of your learning takes place.

Here is a third option for picking the right situation as a target. Think about an upcoming event or meeting on your schedule that's likely to put you in autopilot mode. Look at your calendar and find something where you are likely to lapse into routine, unthinking behaviors and have little sense of your impact on other people. When you see the scheduled event on your calendar, you become anxious, angry or upset in some way, signaling that this may be the perfect situation for you to target with a fresh approach.

Jacki, for instance, tried this technique and discovered that certain types of meetings she had on her schedule made her uncomfortable—they were the meetings where she was in charge. Jacki, a senior level manager for a multi-national company, knew why she was not looking forward to these meetings. In recent months, just about every gathering that she ran ended in acrimonious debate and a lack of closure. With hindsight, she was aware that she would open each meeting with a strongly-worded opinion of what she believed the issue was and what her team should do about it. As a result, the meeting usually turned into a debate about her opinion. It was almost as if she threw down her ideas like gauntlets and challenged everyone to debate her. Therefore, Jacki targeted the next meeting as a chance to test a new behavior—withholding her opinion until the meeting was much further along and others had a chance to voice their views.

Finally, we've created a list of common target situations—ones that frequently cause people distress and have been mentioned repeatedly by individuals going through the ARTT process. Review these situations and see if any of them might become good targets for you:

- A conversation that you don't want to have (i.e. asking for or being asked for a raise, promotion, etc.).

- An encounter with someone who is likely to provide intense pushback or challenge (i.e. you want to suggest that a project be run one way, your team member is adamantly opposed to it being run that way).

- Interactions with people who have a great deal of authority or power.

- An instance where you have to take action (i.e. make a decision) where you possess insufficient or ambiguous information.

- A performance review or any situation where you receive feedback about your attitude, achievements, progress.

- An assignment where a lot is riding on the outcome of your work.

- Any type of situation where you're under the microscope and being evaluated.

- Stretch assignments, such as a task that you've never done before that requires that you use new or undeveloped skills.

- Situations where you're in unfamiliar environments (i.e. working in a foreign country for the first time, being on your first cross-functional team, etc.).

- Presentations to large groups or in tense environments (i.e. a pitch to the CEO for funding for a new program).

While there is some overlap between these situations, you can use this list to see if any of its descriptions create some anxiety in you. It may help you to pinpoint a variation on one of these situations that would be a good target for you to aim at.

A Few More Targeting Tips

As you create your target, you may find that it becomes an abstraction, especially if it is a target that's far off in the distance. Don't set targets that can't be acted upon quickly. The longer you wait, the more difficult it is to keep your target specific and actionable. If you set your target as the company's annual sales meeting six months from now, by the time it rolls around, you will have lost your focus. The target will be out of focus, and you will have allowed equally good targets to pass by without acting. You want your target to be sharply defined in your mind, and with the passing of too much time, it becomes fuzzy around the edges.

Therefore, create targeted situations that will arise within days or weeks, not months.

To keep your target clear and fresh, we also suggest articulating it. One of our earlier exercises involved putting your target in writing. We recognize that for some, creating a written description of a targeted situation may be something you have little time or interest in doing. If this is the case, we urge you to articulate the target verbally to someone you trust who understands you. By talking about the given event or place where you intend to try a new approach, you give it clarity. You don't have to deliver a long speech about your intent. Instead, specify the time and place you're targeting, and the behaviors you are moving away from and the actions you're moving to. This from-to articulation is extremely important, since it allows you to see the difference between your autopilot routines and your new, more aware behaviors.

Finally, we should caution that once you set a target, you may become a bit anxious. This is natural and good. Targeting takes you out of your comfort zone; you're making a commitment to do something in a new way, and that can make you uneasy.

If you feel this way, especially after you articulate your target, remind yourself that you're never going to grow and develop until you take some risks and test some uncomfortable new behaviors. We know that it may feel awkward or be difficult to say or do something in a new way, especially with your colleagues, customers or bosses as witnesses. You may worry about what they're liable to think or say or how they will react to the new you.

> The odds are they'll react well. Remember that there's a reason you're doing things differently in a targeted situation. Your old way of acting isn't getting you anywhere—or it's getting you in trouble. You are creating a learning target in this step, giving yourself a chance to acquire valuable lessons that will increase your effectiveness and enhance your career.

So don't flinch when you create your target. This will help you move forward to the next step, which involves Trying something new.

SKILL SAVVY · SUMMARY

KEY POINTS

- Establish a highly specific target to translate Reflection into behavior change. Zoom in on the specifics of who, what, why and when.

- Targeting prepares you to do and say things differently and keeps you off of autopilot.

- To make your target obtainable, you must believe you can hit it; you must also be motivated to do what it takes to reach your target.

- Good targets are either "follow-up" encounters or situations you would like to avoid --both are times when you are usually on autopilot.

CHAPTER 7

Try: Learning in Action

"The great end of life is not knowledge but action."

— Thomas Henry Huxley, 1877

You can look at this fourth step in the ARTT process from two perspectives. You can view it as the most difficult of the four steps because you actually have to put your self-knowledge and personal understanding into practice. Or you can view this step as the easiest, since it is the culmination of the previous three steps and the payoff for all your preparation.

We see this step as the latter, at least in the sense that you should be well-prepared to apply new, more productive ways of acting in work situations. There's a reason we've spent a lot of time on helping you understand the previous three steps.

> *The Skill* is attainable as part of a process; we could not simply
> tell you to "do this" and expect that you would be able to use
> *the Skill* effectively. It is only after you have become Aware,
> Reflected and Targeted that you're in a position to capitalize
> on what you have learned.

This doesn't mean that when you try a new behavior, everything will go as in a perfect script. As we'll discuss later, the
ARTT process is one that is meant to be repeated, continually
looping on the constant learning and behavior change.

Now, you need to understand how to take this fourth step
with the intended new behavior firmly in mind.

Combining Visualization with Self-Talk

Having targeted a specific business situation where you will test
your new behaviors, you are almost ready to put your self-knowledge into practice. First though, you need to do two exercises
that will increase the odds that things will go according to plan
when you implement your awareness-based actions.

These two exercises involve self-talk and visualization, and
we can best describe what these entail by referring to basket-
ball great Michael Jordan. Before shooting a free throw, Jordan
would go through the same routine. He would dribble the ball
and spin it in his hands. Then he would visualize the correct
way to shoot the free throw. This visualization technique helped
him shoot an unusually high free throw percentage. He could
(and sometimes did) close his eyes and still shoot a free throw
perfectly.

This visualization, though, was not the only thing he did prior
to taking his free throw shots. He was engaged in what we call

self-talk; telling himself to bend his knees, to keep his wrist straight and strong, to look at the inside bolts at the back of the rim.

You can practice self-talk and visualization in a similar manner. Based on your target, rehearse what you're going to say and do, and have a conversation with yourself about what is likely to transpire. During this mental rehearsal, create alternative scenarios based on the choices available to you. Focus on three possible choices you may have at your targeted event. In other words, if you are targeting an upcoming interaction with direct reports and your reflection has revealed that you tend to prevent people from volunteering ideas that are different from your own, you might:

1. Try to talk less and listen more during the first half of the meeting.

2. Try to ask more questions designed to draw out ideas from others.

3. Try to create a more informal atmosphere, holding the discussion off-site, perhaps during lunch, and begin the conversation by talking about your direct report's interests outside of work.

For each scenario, imagine how it might unfold, including both your behaviors and those of your direct report. Visualize both the positive and negative effects, and then talk to yourself about what you're doing that contributes to each type of outcome. Place the scenarios in "if x, then y" terms: If my direct report becomes even more guarded, then I'll have to ask less threatening questions. Think about what you might do to overcome the obstacles you encounter, and if it's feasible to overcome them.

After doing this exercise for each scenario, figure out which one is most likely to provide you with the desired outcome. That's the one you should Try.

What we're advocating is being flexible when thinking about how your upcoming attempt at a new approach might go. Don't lock yourself into one way of trying things, since you really don't know exactly how events will unfold in real time. By visualizing various possibilities and talking to yourself about them, you'll have options for actions to draw upon.

Jobs and careers throw people a lot of curves. What worked yesterday may not work tomorrow. You need to be prepared for changes and surprises. That means giving yourself alternatives for dealing with new situations. For this reason, we are suggesting you practice Trying different approaches and become as adaptable as you can possibly be.

Are You Motivated to Try Something New?

Don't answer this subtitle's question without giving it some thought. Many people believe they are motivated, but the reality is that the desire to change exists only on the surface.

If you half-heartedly want to do something differently, you probably won't try very hard, creatively or consistently. We have found that people become more motivated when they conduct an internal survey about how satisfied they are with their job or their career. By focusing on their performance, promotability and potential—and their satisfaction or lack thereof in each area—they give themselves a reason to try a different approach.

To conduct this survey, use the following questions:

- Am I performing up to my expectations; up to my boss's expectations; up to my clients' or customers' expectations?

- If I'm falling short of expectations, is it by a little bit or a lot? Is there solid evidence that I'm falling short (poor performance reviews, messed-up assignments, etc.)?

- Am I demonstrating skills that make me likely to receive a promotion or plum assignment?

- Do I possess a track record and skills that mark me as a top candidate for jobs at other organizations?

- Am I viewed as a high potential within my organization?

- Am I doing the things necessary to secure a capstone or leadership position down the road?

If these questions raise your level of dissatisfaction, good— your responses will motivate you to try just about anything to be more satisfied with your performance, promotability and potential.

It is also critical that you are specific about what you intend to try. As we mentioned in our Target chapter, it's crucial to define as precisely as possible the event or situation where you will attempt to shift your approach. Just as critical, you need to create highly specific Try behaviors. You may visualize and rehearse three different responses to a situation depending on what happens. Just be sure those responses are specific rather than general. Don't tell yourself, "I'm going to try to be more creative in the meeting." Instead, remind yourself that you are going to "explain my innovative approach to the computer gridlock problem at the very first opportunity in the meeting on Wednesday."

Finally, recognize that a big difference exists between ability and willingness. Most people possess the ability to try new behavior; they are not so rigid that they refuse to consider another approach. Yet though they have the ability, they might not be willing to use it. It is nearly impossible to use *the Skill* effectively if you are unwilling to try new behaviors.

For instance, Steve recognizes that his by-the-numbers approach and no-nonsense demeanor make him seem like a cold fish. He knows he has to loosen up in order to form the relationships necessary to succeed in his organization, and he tells himself that he's going to work at being more casual and communicative. In the heat of battle, though, Steve reverts to his traditional behavior. Because he isn't willing to focus on making changes, he goes back on autopilot.

Research from Lominger International demonstrates how important motivation is. Their studies reveal that 30% of people won't try new behaviors or emerge from their comfort zones. This research also indicates that 55% of people will try new things some of the time, depending on the situation and other factors. Only 10 to 15% regularly try new approaches.

Our suspicion is that the first two groups, which constitute 85% of those surveyed, are not sufficiently motivated.

"Sufficiently motivated" is a key phrase in that it suggests you need more than a passing interest in changing in order to try something new. Therefore, consider the following criteria that we've established for sufficient motivation:

- You believe that there are issues that are making you less effective in your work.

- You accept responsibility for these issues and are convinced you can improve in these areas.

- You want to do something about them now rather than later.

- You have identified an action item and have made a commitment to take the steps the action requires.

The "I Can't Do This" Excuse

It really is an excuse. People erect their own obstacles to trying new, more effective behaviors, and these obstacles often revolve around their inability to act differently. In reality, individuals allow their emotional stress in given situations to "de-skill" them. In other words, they are perfectly capable of being more open and honest or of being more decisive, but when they are under pressure, they revert to autopilot.

Think about the individual who blows up under pressure, who lashes out at direct reports when they miss key deadlines or becomes infuriated with superiors who don't provide the support for big deals that they promised. When he is asked to Try a new, calmer approach in the next high-pressure meeting he runs, he may say, "I can't do that; I don't know how to be that way; people will think it's odd if I try and 'force' a new way of acting."

Yet there are many situations where this person is cool, calm and collected. So he has *the Skill* necessary to handle a tense situation in a controlled manner. It is his emotions and the pressure that de-skill him.

The ARTT process is designed to help people like this identify and prepare for the emotional wave that engulfs them. Once they are aware of the situations where they act counterproductively—once they understand and reflect on the triggers that provoke these negative behaviors—they are in much better positions to deal with them. They can transfer skills they possess (i.e. staying calm, analytical and focused) to targeted situations.

Understand, then, that you don't need to acquire new skills in most instances as part of this process. When you try a new behavior, what you're really doing is transferring a skill you already possess. When you have heightened awareness, you often can perceive when and how you should apply a given skill from your arsenal.

Try, Try, Again!

You can't fail. This should be the mantra of everyone going through the ARTT process. You may temporarily feel awkward or even embarrassed, but that's good. When you move out of your comfort zone, you should experience these feelings. When you find yourself struggling as you try to say or do something differently, that's a sign that you're learning through the loop. And "double-loop learning" is what ARTT is all about.

Be aware, though, that when you try something new, you must debrief yourself. As later chapters will demonstrate, you're going to recycle through the four steps of ARTT repeatedly. That is what we mean by double-loop learning. For our purposes here, though, focus on debriefing yourself after you try something new. Specifically, ask yourself:

1.What went well?
2.What didn't go well?
3.What will I do differently the next time?

Now, you may notice these questions are the same "what" questions from the first step of becoming Aware. This makes your effort at trying a new approach worthwhile. If you try something and ignore the result or beat yourself up if it doesn't go well, you've learned nothing. If you use your "from-to" technique properly, on the other hand, you'll gain insights into how you behave in a given situation—what works and what doesn't when you move from x to y. This is invaluable information the next time the situation rolls around again.

Keep in mind all the ways you can learn from a "trying experience": For instance, here are some examples of key observations and learnings you might extract when you debrief after the situation.

- You discover that you tried too hard. You were overly dramatic in your attempt at a new approach; it didn't seem natural to people. You talked too loudly, were too quiet or too assertive. You went overboard. Next time you know to moderate the new behavior.

- You realize you were too subtle. Some people are tentative about trying. They think that their behaviors varied radically from the norm, but in fact they altered their ways of acting so slightly that no one noticed. During debriefing, this learning will help you ratchet it up a notch.

- You see yourself as others see you. Most of us are oblivious to our effect on other people, in part because we are always the same and so we don't pay much attention on how others react (because they always seem to react in the same way). When we vary our style or substance, however, it usually stimulates a reaction. You may cause others to ask more questions, they may be more friendly. They may be more willing to confide in you. This is great learning for relationship building.

- You give yourself ideas about what to try next time. Trying a new type of behavior is tricky in that, if it doesn't go perfectly the first time, you're not sure what to do the second time. Your debriefing will provide you with behavioral alternatives. You may think to yourself that next time you should wait longer before you say or do something. Or you may find that in the next situation, you'll focus your attention and actions on one individual, rather than spreading yourself too thin.

In short, you gain alternative ideas for
taking action when you cycle through
ARTT again.

Finally, remember this fourth step involves not what you did
as much as how you did it. Concentrate on the how, and as you
cycle through ARTT, the what will come naturally.

SKILL SAVVY SUMMARY

TRY: LEARNING IN ACTION

KEY POINTS

- Mentally rehearse how you will act in the targeted situation, including what you will do if things do not go as planned.

- Develop techniques that "buy time" so that you can reflect when you encounter unexpected obstacles.

- Remember to debrief with yourself after you try new behaviors. After your action experience is over, base your self-talk in reality while debriefing by asking: What went well; what did not go well; what will I do differently in the future?

CHAPTER 8

The Cycling Phenomenon

"Practice makes perfect."
— John Adams, personal diary, 1761

Cycling through the four steps of ARTT requires a conscious, consistent effort. People sometimes use the process to achieve short-term goals rather than make it part of their modus operandi. As a result, they may utilize the four steps one or even a few times, but eventually revert back to their old, subconscious behaviors.

Our clients sometimes ask how many times they need to cycle through ARTT for it to be effective, and we respond that they are asking the wrong question. It's not as if a magic number exists—five times through ARTT and your targeted behavior gets permanently added to your arsenal of skills. Instead, cycling through the four steps needs to become a lifelong habit, a method of continuous learning and improvement.

As easy as it is to write the previous statement, it can be challenging to put this approach into practice, especially given the times in which we live and work.

The Quick Fix Mentality

Too often, people apply ARTT as a short-term solution to immediate problems. At a time when pressure is intense and people have done all they can do to keep their heads above water, they gravitate toward anything that will provide instant relief. Many professionals we talk to refer to the need to get through the day or the week; they have difficulty thinking in terms of months or years.

Though this mentality is a product of a short-term results environment, it isn't what ARTT is all about. If you use ARTT just to survive a difficult conversation with your boss, your fix may be quick and get you through, but it will also only be temporary. If you fail to keep cycling through ARTT, you won't learn anything from the fix; you're bound to have more difficult conversations not only with your boss, but with customers, colleagues and others, and even if you use ARTT occasionally, you will only be realizing marginal results and using a fraction of its power. Continually cycling through ARTT allows you to transfer what you learn to your behaviors. If you are wanting to make changes to your behavior for the long term, you have to stay committed to cycling through ARTT.

To avoid using ARTT as a quick fix, be aware of the three common reasons that people stop cycling through ARTT:

- **They solve a problem.** In effect, ARTT worked too well. They use ARTT to deal with a particular behavior that's causing them difficulties in work situations. They have a big client meeting in a week, and want to make sure they display the more positive attitude that the client wanted to see from their service provider. Or they are eager to demonstrate to their direct reports that they can be kinder and gentler during performance reviews, so they use ARTT to achieve this goal when they do their next four reviews. This single-minded focus on solving one problem is short-sighted. Just as alarmingly, people will invariably revert to old behaviors after they stop using ARTT.

- **They believe they no longer have a need for it.** For instance, a given person may go through three or four cycles of ARTT, become more conscious of their behaviors and try new ones successfully. Though they didn't use ARTT to solve a specific external problem, they wanted it to change internal attitudes or behaviors. Now, they believe they are permanently fixed. In fact, self-awareness is never a given. It takes consistent effort to avoid slipping back into auto-pilot mode.

- **The quick fix doesn't work.** You go through the four steps in anticipation of creating new, improved capabilities in a matter of weeks,

and when you test a new behavior in a key
situation, you fail to achieve anticipated
results. Perhaps you find yourself unable to
try a new behavior—you revert to your old
way of doing things. Perhaps you are able to
do something differently, but it ends up with
the same mediocre results. Consequently,
you throw away ARTT like a broken tool.

It is possible that ARTT will not yield the precise result you
want the first time you use it... or the second or third times. It
took you a while to behave the way you do, and it may take a
while for you to adopt a new, more productive behavior. In the
interim, though, recognize that it's impossible for ARTT to fail.
Even when you don't get the desired results, you obtain great
learning each time you employ it. Debriefing yourself after every
Try allows you to access critical feedback. You learn a lot about
yourself, and this learning will help you the next time you're in
a similar situation. It will help, that is, if you continue to cycle
through ARTT, reapplying the newly acquired learnings.

The good news is that if you can overcome this quick fix
mentality, the process itself motivates continued cycling through
the four steps. Once you achieve a big "win"—you change a
behavior in a way that helps you receive a coveted promotion or
your team reaches a major objective—you want to keep using
ARTT in anticipation of future big wins.

ARTT is a Way of Life

When people first begin using ARTT, they often take a situational
perspective. They see it as a tool that will help them deal more
effectively with challenging work situations—customer meetings,

client presentations and so on. It is fine to start out with this situational thinking, but you should also think in broader terms about how it can change your behavior in all situations.

This doesn't mean that it takes years to benefit from ARTT, only that the benefits become more significant the more you cycle through. It is important to keep in mind that ARTT helps you use dormant skills or capacities in a full range of situations. It requires continuous usage for you to use these skills effectively, and it requires more time and practice until you can use them in more than one specific situation. Continually cycling through the four steps, therefore, is the way you can get the most out of the process.

If you recall our story about Jacki from Chapter 6, she was the corporate manager who tended to dominate her meetings by expressing her ideas early on, effectively preventing others from participating in meaningful ways. She Targeted a meeting to Try a new approach where she let others express their ideas before she expressed her viewpoint.

Her approach worked and soon her weekly project management sessions yielded much more innovative ideas and accomplished a lot more than in the past. Jacki saw how her team was able to construct clear, realistic objectives and achieve them because of her new way of leading these meetings. Happy about the results she had achieved through ARTT, she resolved to keep cycling through the steps, not just in morning meetings, but in other situations.

Jacki became aware that she was not particularly adept at influencing her boss' decisions regarding finances and resource allocations for her group's projects. She Reflected on why it was this way and realized that though she was driven and ambitious, she was not particularly politically savvy and this hampered her communications with her boss. Therefore, she set Targets for improving this skill and began trying out new behaviors in these situations—she amazed herself at how well she learned to read the politically delicate problems her boss had to resolve before she could give one group more resources than another. As Jacki cycled through ARTT, she picked up on managerial nuances and gradually became a much more influential manager. In fact, soon her influence extended past her boss to her boss' boss.

Even more enthusiastic about her continuous learning process than before, Jacki became a disciple of ARTT. After a while, she used the four steps consistently, relying on them not only to deal with specific situations, but as a way to improve her performance and effectiveness. After a year, Jacki knew that she was a different manager than she had been pre-ARTT. The signs were everywhere: her boss relied on her more than in the past, colleagues called her frequently with questions and requests for her to work with their teams, the CEO even included Jacki on an elite strategic task force.

Within two years, Jacki had received a significant promotion as well as a tempting offer (which she turned down) to join a competitor.

Let Learning be Your Guide

If you're like most people, you're wondering what the experience of cycling through ARTT constantly is like. How do you know you are making progress during those periods where instantaneous results are not tangibly seen? How can you be sure that you are not focusing on one step too much and another step too little? What if you're repeatedly trying and failing to cycle through ARTT and incorporate a behavior? How many cycles does it take before you see a change in your behavior or the positive results you want?

These are difficult questions to answer in the general sense, since the answer that is right for you may not apply to someone else. Everyone learns and changes at different speeds. As we have noted, some people have deep-seated emotional issues and hidden pain they need to overcome before they can change. Others are in dicey work situations and may need to apply what they learn in other environments to see results.

We recognize that these qualifications won't satisfy your desire to know where in the cycling process you are. For that reason, we recommend using learning as a way of measuring your progress. Specifically, ask yourself the following questions as you cycle through the steps:

- What insights have I gained about myself from what just took place (in a meeting, presentation, conversation, etc.)?

- Could I have misinterpreted some insights about myself? Do I need to test my insights?

- Have I discovered a specific attitude or behavioral problem that leads me to be less effective in this setting than I want to be?

- When I try to act differently and don't get a good result, why is that? What am I doing that is preventing me from achieving this result?

- Is my failure at trying a result of setting my target too high? Am I trying to do too much too soon? Should I set a more realistic target?

- When I try something new and succeed (or partially succeed), why has my new approach been more effective than my traditional one?

- Am I consistently able to apply what I've learned when similar situations occur?

- Am I consistently able to apply what I've learned in a wide variety of situations?

- Has my learning helped bring out dormant skills that I didn't realize I possessed?

- Have I received a promotion or other type of reward that is directly attributable to the knowledge I gained through the ARTT process?

- Am I now viewed within the organization (or outside of it) as a more qualified candidate for higher level jobs because of how my learning has impacted my management or leadership approach?

You're not going to be able to answer all these questions affirmatively until you've cycled through ARTT multiple times. That's fine. Learning takes place in stages, so it may take a bit of time until you figure out how to apply the insights you've gained.

Remember too, that your self-learning can be a tricky proposition. As we noted in earlier chapters, sometimes you can act a certain way in certain situations because of emotionally painful experiences in your past. Coming to terms with these experiences isn't as matter-of-fact as it sounds when described on the page. In fact, it can be messy. The first few times you cycle through ARTT, you may be in denial about what you're doing wrong; you may cling to your routine because it's difficult to acknowledge the traps you fall into during conflict with colleagues or when your boss is overly demanding.

That's why it is so important to repeat the steps of ARTT. Even the most stubborn, self-denying individual usually gets it after hitting his head against the wall five times. For instance, the first time you go through ARTT, part of you may be convinced that you are not close-minded when high-risk, high-reward options are suggested. The second time through the cycle, you may be skeptical about your close-mindedness. The third time, you may at least entertain the possibility. The fourth time, you may try a new, less close-minded behavior and realize that it's probable rather than possible that you haven't been open to innovative ideas. The fifth time, you may decide to embrace a riskier approach and see it pay off. Now it becomes apparent how limiting your close-mindedness was to your development and your career.

Learning takes time, but it is a good measure for how your cycling is progressing. It may not be as "clean" a progression as the previous example suggests. You may go through three or four cycles and become more aware of this close-mindedness, but then something happens during the fourth cycle to return you to a skeptical mindset. In other words, two steps forward, one step back might mark your learning.

That's okay, as long as you see yourself climbing the learning curve over time.

Measure how Your Learning Translates into Behaviors

Quality trumps quantity when it comes to cycling through ARTT. You don't earn extra credit based on the number of times you cycle through the four steps. While you want to move through them consistently, you don't want to set numerical goals like 100 cycles per year.

Instead, focus on behavioral changes. If you lost your temper 90% of the time during high-stress meetings in the past, what is the percentage after cycling through ARTT consistently for three months? For six months? For nine months? Ideally, you are seeing the percentage of negative behaviors diminish incrementally. Each time you go through the four steps, you obtain an insight or gain some perspective that should translate into more productive work actions.

While some of these behavioral changes will be obvious and measurable, others will be subtle. From week to week, you may not be able to see how you are growing more perceptive about how to get things done in your organization or how you are developing into a more authoritative leader. Nonetheless, the cycling process produces this growth and development over time, and you should note evidence that it is taking place. This evidence may be as obvious as a promotion from your boss and the comment that you've "become a much better decision-maker in recent months," or it may take the form of more colleagues asking you for advice or to participate with them on a project.

By being responsive to this positive feedback, you reinforce your motivation to continue to cycle through ARTT.

SKILL SAVVY SUMMARY

THE CYCLING PHENOMENON

KEY POINTS

- The use of ARTT is more than a one-time fix. It is the beginning of your acquisition of *the Skill*. Remember to use it time and time again.

- The more frequently you use ARTT, the less often you will be on autopilot.

- Your early efforts may not yield the results you want. However, you cannot fail, as long as you learn from your efforts. Keep reflecting and targeting your learnings. Never give up.

- Monitor your progress by asking yourself questions and asking others for feedback.

CHAPTER 9

The Early Warning System

"The pause that refreshes."

— Coca-Cola,
Advertising Slogan, 1929

> Autopilot may sound benign, but it can have a devastating impact on everything from your decision-making to your leadership. Without knowing it, you can slip into autopilot mode, failing to recognize that your behaviors have become rigid and predictable. Even though we warn our clients to keep alert for the autopilot trap, sometimes they are caught unaware. Unless you're vigilant, you can end up falling back into old, unthinking routines, especially when you are going through a difficult transition.

As you read about cycling through the four steps of ARTT, it may have seemed perfectly logical and easy to implement.

We've tried to show the ideal way in which ARTT works and how you can use it to benefit from whatever challenges and opportunities you encounter. In the real world, though, the process can be less logical and more emotional. Despite your best efforts, you may find yourself responding to a boss, a customer or a colleague in ways you know are counterproductive. Despite following ARTT religiously, you fall back on your old, unconscious reflexes when you're under stress or dealing with difficult people.

As you may have noticed, one of our themes is that slipping back into autopilot mode is a danger for everyone. Though you may tell yourself that you're not going to slip, you're not always in conscious control of your responses. Deep felt emotions that are anchored in past negative experiences can trigger behaviors that, if we were fully aware, our mind would censure. In the heat of the moment, though, we are likely just to react without much thinking.

To prevent this from happening, we'd like to offer a tool we call the Early Warning System (EWS). It is designed to raise your awareness of the situations, people or events most likely to throw you back into autopilot mode, sounding an alarm in your head when you are on the cusp of acting in an unaware manner.

How and Why EWS Works

Imagine if you had a yellow warning light that flashed in your head whenever you were about to engage in counterproductive work behaviors or a siren that sounded when you started engaging in these behaviors. EWS serves essentially the same function, albeit without the sensory power of actual lights or alarms.

Let's say that you're talking with your boss, and he says that you're falling short of his expectations and letting your team down. You're vulnerable to any criticism from a boss, but especially criticism that involves letting people down. Your first reaction is to respond defensively, to list all your accomplishments in the last month, to detail how you enabled your team to meet a critical goal and so on. While it's possible that you are absolutely right and your boss is absolutely wrong, you lack the ability to make an objective judgment about this issue. You snap so quickly into autopilot mode that you are not aware of your vulnerability. Rather than reflecting, you're just reacting.

However, if you would have had an EWS in place, you would have stopped yourself from reacting in this way. Beforehand, you would have created a list of your autopilot triggers, one of which in this case would be an authority figure telling you that you've fallen short of expectations. You would have also charted your typical response to this trigger - intense defensiveness and heated denial - and you would have created a mechanism to alert yourself that you were engaged in this autopilot response. Perhaps you listed three common signs: making "opening statements" like a lawyer defending a client; feeling your face flush and your fingers drumming on a table; refusing to let anyone else speak.

All this alerts you that you are in danger of slipping back into autopilot mode. This alert is often enough to prevent any slippage. The danger is always reacting without thinking, and this danger is especially acute when you are under stress or in a "triggering" situation—a particular set of circumstances that evoke powerful feelings.

As part of your EWS, we strongly recommend creating a list of triggering situations. Based on research from the Centre of

Creative Leadership, we've adapted the following list of situations that are commonly challenging and stressful.

- A work project with a high probability of failure
- A boss or other influential person with whom you have "personality conflicts"
- Deadline pressure involving important projects
- A stretch assignment
- A new job or new position (transfer, job promotion, etc.)
- A crisis (potential loss of big customer, lawsuit, etc.)
- Adjusting to a new boss
- Implementing a major new process or policy
- Requirement to climb a steep learning curve

While there may be some overlap between two or more of these triggers, you'll find it useful to keep them in mind and know which ones in particular you are vulnerable to. In this way, you give yourself one more tool to help activate the EWS before your autopilot switches on.

Keep in mind that an EWS is an alert system, and as such, it can have a variety of components that function together. For instance, you may designate a colleague as someone to point out to you when you're acting in a reflexive, unconscious manner. Perhaps you've asked your direct report to tap a pencil on a cup whenever you act a certain way in staff meetings. This is simply an additional external warning to back up your own internal warning system.

Some people, of course, don't want to ask another person to serve as this external warning system, either because they don't feel comfortable asking anyone to fill this role or because no one person is usually around them and able to warn them. For this reason, cueing images are often the preferred external warning tool.

Taking a Cue from an Object

A cueing image can be any object that helps warn you that you're slipping into autopilot mode. While you may believe that you can warn yourself via internal devices, most people benefit from the back-up of an external object of some sort.

For instance, some of our clients have used their wristwatch as a cueing device. When Robert meets with his team, he reflexively steers the conversation away from risky but innovative ideas. Regardless of whether an idea has merit, Robert becomes nervous when something "new and different" is mentioned. Though he recognizes the value of innovation and taking reasonable risks, something inside of him finds a way to sabotage any discussion that involves these topics.

To prevent himself from doing so, Robert puts his watch on his right wrist (he usually wears it on his left wrist) prior to these meetings. All it takes is a glance down at his hands and the unnatural sight of the watch on the "wrong" wrist for Robert to hear the warning: don't shy away from innovative proposals! The unusual sight of the watch on the wrong hand is just enough to jar him out of his unaware state and allow him the awareness necessary to cycle through ARTT.

The cueing device functions like a Post-it note. It is a re-
minder to do something that, in the heat of the moment or the
routine of the day, you might otherwise forget. In fact, one of
my clients actually put a Post-it note in a notebook he brought to
every meeting, glancing at the note periodically to remind him
of the danger of falling back into autopilot. Though we'll leave
the choice of a cueing object to your imagination, we'd like to
give you some suggestions about how to link cues with specific
behaviors. Here are some sample links:

- Autopilot behavior: Becoming indecisive when faced
  with numerous options for action
- Cueing device: A small courtroom gavel, signifying
  that decisions must be made

- Autopilot behavior: Analysis paralysis during planning
  sessions
- Cueing device: A piece of paper with lots of facts and
  figures on it, with a big X superimposed over the data

- Autopilot behavior: Relying on intelligence without
  empathy when doing performance reviews
- Cueing device: A framed photo of daughter when she
  was a two-year-old

We should add that the cueing device doesn't have to be
related to the behavior as clearly as these four objects are. In
our earlier example, the wristwatch had nothing to do with the
negative autopilot behavior. The key is to choose something
that will snag your attention and remind you to cease and desist
from the subconscious behavior toward which you're drifting.

The Power of Pausing

Think about how you act when you visit your parents or any relatives with whom you've grown up. As soon as you see them, you probably revert to old ways of behaving. You may not want to act this way; your spouse may have even told you how irritating it is when you become a little boy again when you visit your mom. But when you see these family members, the weight of all those years together throws you back into old routines.

A similar response occurs when you lapse into autopilot at work. You can tell yourself 100 times that you can no longer micromanage eight direct reports, yet as soon as there's an important project and you feel Joe and Jill aren't doing their tasks the right way, you step in and do their work for them. It's an unthinking reflex, and it's so powerful in part because it may have helped you meet deadlines and achieve goals in the past. It's become a habit, and it's a difficult habit to break.

An Early Warning System is a way to help you break this habit. If you recall from Chapter 4, we discussed the concept of "hitting pause." When your EWS is in good working order, it helps you pause the action, opening up a window for you to use ARTT. As soon as you make yourself Aware, you have a decent chance of keeping your autopilot off and being in full control of how you act in a given situation.

Of course, you can't literally pause a meeting or a conversation, but you can give yourself that micro-second in your mind where you step back and observe your own behavior.

When your EWS sounds the alarm, you possess the power to gain some perspective on what's going inside your head and the actions taking place outside of it. It is an opportunity to do something differently, to stop yourself from making a decision you'll later regret or failing to say something that should be said.

EWS gives you this opportunity. As we'll learn, self-talk is what sustains and directs the opportunity, ensuring you stay off autopilot.

SKILL SAVVY SUMMARY

THE EARLY WARNING SYSTEM

KEY POINTS

- You can slip into autopilot in a fraction of a second. Stress can cause you to revert to old behaviors, unaware of your choices.

- Develop a yellow caution light (Early Warning System) so that you can hit pause and ratchet up your awareness. This "hitting pause" can be done in real time (rather than after the fact).

- Use an external object or cue as your Early Warning System. Choose a cue that is going to capture your attention and do a good job of warning you of going on autopilot.

- When you pause, you have the opportunity to choose a different course of action.

- Your early warning system triggers the reality based self-talk that keeps you off of auto-pilot and helps you be more effective, skillful and learning-focused.

CHAPTER 10

Reality-Based Self-Talk

"When one is in love, one always begins by deceiving
one's self, and ends by deceiving others."
— Oscar Wilde,
The Picture of Dorian Gray, 1891

Just as the Early Warning System is a tool to keep you moving through ARTT, reality-based self-talk serves a similar purpose.

Rather than alerting you when you're about to return to autopilot, reality-based self-talk keeps you anchored to what is really taking place—both inside and outside of your head. This is critical, since ARTT won't work if you are mired in false negativity and the unconscious pain from your past. Typically, after your EWS has made you aware that you are slipping into an old, counterproductive routine, you start hearing words running through your mind. If you're able to regulate what you are saying to yourself—if you can focus on what is really going on and what you can learn from it—then you'll be able to Reflect effectively.

Essentially, reality-based self-talk allows you to listen to yourself clearly. This clarity of reception can make all the difference in whether you learn and grow from ARTT or become sidetracked. Though you may have heard the term, "self-talk" before, we need to look at it as a reality-based tool and within the context of ARTT.

Two Types of Self-Talk

Everyone has a voice inside his or her head. Some people refer to it as their conscience. Some view it as a commentator on whatever is occurring in their lives. Others describe it as an internal critic, constantly pointing out what they or others did wrong. They perceive it to be a hindrance, rather than a help, something they would like to shut off like an irritatingly loud motor.

For some people, this voice is inaudible. It is so rooted in the subconscious that they don't hear it. Or it is so weighted with emotion that they don't want to hear it. Or they simply perceive the voice as "thinking" and don't separate it out and really listen to what it is saying. But it is still just as powerful, and often has strong influence on their decisions.

It is important to listen to and self-regulate it; that's how you can learn from your internal voice and incorporate it into the ARTT process. First, though, we should divide self-talk into two simple categories: good and bad. Good self-talk is based in reality and objective. You analyze events perceptively and ask yourself questions designed to extract the learning from an event. You attempt to get at the essence of what you did and what it means.

Bad self-talk, on the other hand, is largely about blaming others and is rooted in self-deception. The voice in your head focuses on how others wronged you, what they did to you and why they were wrong. This is as opposed to concentrating on what is happening to you, what you were responsible for, what you can change about your behavior and the reality of your situation.

You possess the power to regulate this self-talk. You don't have to allow it to unspool in your mind like an unedited tape. Instead, you can refocus your internal monologue so that it is about a search for meaning, self-assessment and personal responsibility.

The first thing you need to know in order to regulate your self-talk, is the difference between the good and bad kind. The following chart will help in that regard:

Good Self-talk (Reality-Based)	Bad Self-talk (Self-Deceived)
• What could I have done to frame this so that we could make a decision?	• The rest of the team never makes decisions in these meetings.
• I wonder what I did that caused her to say that.	• I can't believe she said that to me; I wasn't the one responsible for the loss of that customer.
• What information can I give them to help them understand the situation?	• They don't know what they are talking about.
• Could I have been more specific in my communication?	• He always gets lost in the details.
• How can I connect with people who disagree with me?	• I am not talking to him about it – he is always on the wrong side of the issue.
• What is really going on with him – what does he really mean?	• He always says one thing – but means another.
• What can I do to assist her to help get this done?	• She doesn't deliver – this won't get done.

As you can see from this table, bad self-talk often focuses on what someone else said or did that causes problems. Scapegoating is a common theme of this negative monologue. So too is a focus on the incompetence or inadequacy of others.

Good self-talk may revolve around problematic situations, but the monologue isn't blame-focused. It concentrates on learning and understanding. The questions that often comprise this type of self-talk are designed to figure out what you might do differently in a similar situation to produce a better outcome or to try to understand the other person. Good self-talk is primarily driven by asking yourself questions, not by making judgmental statements. Recognize too, that self-talk doesn't arrive in neat little boxes and fully-formed sentences such as those pictured here. If you don't listen closely, you may hear only snippets of this self-talk. Even if you listen closely, self-talk may emerge more as a stream of a conscious flow of words versus perfectly coherent thoughts. Therefore, what you need to do is give order and coherence to these thoughts. What are you really saying to yourself? Are you asking yourself questions without blaming anyone? Or is your self-talk angry and accusatory?

It may help if you "transcribe" what the voice running through your head is saying. When you sense that your self-talk is occurring—usually after a difficult conversation or meeting—listen carefully and try and write out what you are saying concisely and clearly. For instance, you may be hearing something like: "I can't believe it...Fred did the same thing before and we had a long talk. He made the same stupid mistake, I warned him. The other day, over lunch, right before Jim stopped and said hello, and Jim might have at least had the guts to back me up later that day when I asked Fred to stop giving excuses...I just can't believe he thinks he can get away with it. He's like a child."

You can extrapolate out of this self-talk the following: "Fred made the same mistake. It was stupid, and I warned him about it. Jim acted like a coward. I asked Fred to stop making excuses, but he's like a child."

In the same way, you want to transcribe good self-talk. Be careful, though, that you don't arbitrarily turn statements into questions. When you know the way you "should" be talking to yourself, you may unconsciously upgrade your blaming statements into positive questions. Remember, this isn't a test. You're not going to be able to move from negative to positive self-talk unless you're honest with yourself. Going back to our example of Fred, good self-talk would look like: "What role did I play in the situation? Was I clear in my communication to Fred?"

We should also emphasize that your self-talk is going to vary based on circumstance. Some events are more stressful than others, and in those situations you are more likely to blame others and make other negative comments than in ones where you feel in control. Accept, therefore, that at times you may do a better job of being in a learning, questioning state of mind than others. The key here, though, is to understand what your self-talk consists of and identify patterns, determining when you engage in the good self-talk and when you engage in the bad type.

Assess Your Vulnerability

Some people are more prone to negative self-talk than others. It helps if you're aware if you have these tendencies, since it helps you be more vigilant about identifying it and changing it. We've found that in worst case scenarios, negative self-talkers refuse to acknowledge that they engage in internal monologues where they don't take responsibility for their own actions by blaming others. Even if you're not at this extreme, you should locate yourself on a continuum and know how likely you're going to be to engage in the wrong kind of self-talk.

To that end, rate yourself according to the following seven statements by using the scale provided:

Self Talk – Reality Screening

1. I give advice to others and often follow the same advice.

2. I know explicitly what I should do (or not do) and do it!

3. When talking to others, my reactions, assessments, and observations are in line with other people's perceptions of me.

4. I am aware of my own areas of biased thought in discussions and raise awareness of it to myself and others.

5. I am able to withhold judgments when observing; I gather information and consider alternative explanations and decisions.

6. When I reflect on situations I am able not only to recall specifics of what others did and said, but am able to see my role and the impact I had.

7. When faced with doing something new, I am relaxed and willing to do it; I do not struggle with anxiety or feelings of inadequacy.

–Self Talk Scales–

For each Question rate yourself by the following scale according to the frequency you exhibit the behaviors in the statement:

1	2	3	4	5
Not at all	Rarely	Sometimes	Often	Most of the Time

Sum of all 7 Questions

30-35 = Often utilizes reality based self-talk

25-29 = Willing to engage in self-enquiry

19-24 = Situationally uses reality based self-talk

13-18 = At times, can be deceived

12 and Below = Highly vulnerable to deceiving self-talk

If you scored 12 or below, you probably are the sort of person who likely struggles with deceptive self-talk; whose perceptions of situations are very different from your colleagues; who is judgmental and is blind to your role, especially when things go wrong; and who feels inferior and nervous even when you hold a position of influence.

The odds are you aren't in the highly vulnerable category. Most people fall into the middle three groups, which means you exhibit some of these negative self-talk traits, some of the time. That's fine. The key is to recognize these facts—to face the realities—and then begin regulating your self-talk and ground it more in reality. If you scored under 18 and are vulnerable to self-deceptive self-talk you need to disciple yourself to ask more questions of yourself.

Consider "installing" an Early Warning System to alert you to your negative self-talk. When you catch yourself judging harshly or unfairly, hit pause and transition your self-talk to beneficial, reality-based self-talk. Ask yourself the behavioral questions that allow you determine what you were really responsible for.

The Goal is Self-Regulation

What good does all this self-talk knowledge do? It allows you to monitor how your emotions and bias are impacting your behavior in work situations. Most people are only dimly aware of how their negative self-talk causes them to treat direct reports poorly, to create bad impressions on bosses and to be less effective in many different ways.

If you recall, in Chapter 4 we introduced the concept of the Pain Lump. Not only does it incite fear and hold us hostage to emotions, the pain lump also impacts our self-talk. If it is allowed free rein, it pushes people to do and say things that are not in their best interest—or the best interest of the company.

When you are aware of your self-talk, however, you also become aware of this Pain Lump and its impact. Your self-talk is a direct reflection of this lump; if you're speaking about others resentfully and angrily, it probably has something to do with an emotionally difficult experience in your past.

Once your Early Warning System allows you to hit pause and you become Aware of the self-talk spooling through your mind, you can Reflect on what this monologue is all about and think about where it is coming from. Why are you always blaming one direct report for all the problems your group is experiencing? Why are you always telling your boss off in your interior conversations?

You don't have to be a psychologist to answer these questions. You need to be a veteran of ARTT, and that simply means taking the time to reflect on why your self-talk takes the form that it does and how it affects your attitude and behaviors. This reflection will enable you to regulate what you say to yourself, shifting the conversation to a more questioning, positive, reality-based mode.

Let's say that you set up a meeting with your boss to discuss a few concerns about your role in the organization, and at the last second, he cancels the meeting. This is the second time he's done this in the past month, and your emotional letdown fuels your self-talk. Growing up, you felt let down by your father, a busy corporate lawyer who often had to disappoint you because of his long hours. As a result, your self-talk goes something like this:

My boss doesn't really value me or else he wouldn't cancel these meetings. He's too important to bother with me; he doesn't care what I have to say. He wouldn't do this to John or Mary. But he figures it doesn't matter what I think. I might as well start looking for another job before he gets rid of me.

The odds are that none of this is real. Even worse, you may not even realize that this is the conversation going on in your head. You may find yourself applying for and taking another job that isn't as good as the one you currently have, all because of this unacknowledged and unexamined self-talk.

When your Early Warning System sounds though, you become aware of what you are saying to yourself and start thinking about it. The more you reflect on it, the more you realize that there is an explanation for what took place. You recall your boss telling you that the past month has been incredibly busy; that he had told you that he might be called to an emergency client meeting this week; that two weeks ago he emailed you and communicated how much he appreciated your work on a key project and how it really helped the team and the organization.

This knowledge allows you to regulate your self-talk and avoid making a major career mistake. More importantly, it builds a required tool which is foundational to effectively cycling through ARTT. It ensures that you continue to keep learning and growing.

SKILL SAVVY SUMMARY

REALITY-BASED SELF-TALK

KEY POINTS

- Good self-talk is determined by asking questions about yourself.

- Bad self-talk is when you find yourself judging other people's behaviors.

- It is all about you. You are responsible for your behavior.

- Self-talk is the mechanism that drives your self-awareness and gives you the power to regulate your own behavior.

CHAPTER 11

The Leader: Why Organizations will Demand High Performers Who can Learn and Adapt

"Leading by example isn't simply the best way,
it is the only way."

— Vince Lombardi, Head Coach of the
Green Bay Packers, 1962

The definition of leadership is changing. The old notion of a leader as a decisive, authoritative military type has faded fast.

Organizations are recognizing that the rigidity of this traditional leadership model is no longer relevant in today's world. Yes, leaders still need to be decisive and exercise authority in certain situations, but it's even more important that they are able to learn and adapt their approach as situations change.

Having *the Skill* is critical for achieving this goal, and ARTT provides a process to obtain it. While leaders have always had to deal with transitions, these transitions will only increase in number and difficulty in the future. Any leader who is unaware, who is locked into one behavioral mode, who isn't Reflective and who doesn't Target and Try new behaviors will have trouble surviving in a changing environment. The level of ambiguity, speed, uncertainty and volatility in most workplaces is going to increase, and any leader on autopilot is going to struggle to find new, more effective ways of operating in these environments.

Leaders who self-inquire and continuously learn and adapt by using ARTT, on the other hand, will be capable of handling all sorts of new processes, assignments and cultures effectively. Think of ARTT as a way to integrate new ideas and insights,and produce fresh approaches based on this integration. Integrated systems are the wave of the future, whether you are talking about cell phones with their integrated features of email, phone, data, music, photos and more, or you are talking about leadership. People who integrate knowledge of their past patterns and problems with Awareness of and Reflection on current situations will possess a huge advantage. Like an avid cell phone user, they'll have more capabilities at their fingertips.

To understand how this is so, let's look at the traits that will be absolutely essential for leaders in the coming years and how ARTT integrates these traits into one "system."

The Ten Traits of "Skilled" Leaders

In the old days, leadership traits included strategic ability, analytical skills, decisiveness, motivational skills, conflict resolution and so on. We're not suggesting these traits will be unimportant in the future, only that they won't be as critical as the following list:

- **Self-Awareness.**

    Leaders who don't know themselves are incapable of learning and growing. They may be very smart and competent, but when they are faced with changing situations, they are stuck in their ruts. Self-awareness provides a pathway for business leaders to adapt their approaches, knowing where they need to change. Imagine a company that is acquired not once but twice in five years, and the second acquisition results in new ownership whose style and philosophy are light years removed from what a leader is used to. The transition to this new style will be difficult for everyone, but leaders with acute self-awareness can quickly see how old behaviors aren't working in the new environment and change their approach accordingly.

- **Openness**

    Leaders used to rely on a small cadre of like-minded advisors and tended to follow conventional wisdom. This homogeneous perspective isn't particularly effective in a diverse culture where people are encouraged to think outsideof the box. The ARTT process frees leaders from their narrow thinking. It helps them see that the way they perceive people or ideas may be rooted in an emotional incident from their past; it helps them to see what is going on around them through new clear lens and try fresh ways of doing things based on that reflection. ARTT is a mind-opening process, helping people to listen seriously to what other people are saying as well as what they are saying to themselves.

- **Drive**

Leaders can no longer rest on their laurels, and the impetus to grow and develop will be even stronger in the coming years. ARTT is one of the best ways to achieve this goal. The bar is going to be raised higher for all leaders, and the only way to meet raised expectations will be through internal development. It is great to take executive leadership courses and work harder than in the past, but these efforts will result in a relatively small increase in productivity. The essence of ARTT is continuous improvement; you are always cycling through the process, learning new skills and reshaping attitudes and behaviors.

- **Inquisitiveness**

To gather a diverse set of ideas, leaders often need to be pro-active. They can't just wait for people to volunteer fresh thinking, but must draw it out of them. Self-aware people aren't content to rely on established procedures and policies; they aren't set in their ways. They want to target new ways of doing things. By seeking out new ideas and asking questions, they are better able to do so.

- **Discipline**

Time is in short supply today, and every trend suggests that it will be in shorter supply tomorrow. Highly conscious leaders are not disorganized dreamers. On the contrary, the ARTT process requires discipline and adds it to your leadership arsenal. It offers four steps that leaders can use in every aspect of their work lives. Pie-in-the-sky thinking is not part of these four steps. Instead, it suggests concentrating on specific actions in order to generate results.

• Determination

We don't want to paint a doom-and-gloom picture of the future, but given increased competition in a global marketplace, diminishing natural resources and political upheaval, leaders are going to have their hands full. Just about every leader is going to face more crises than in the past, whether it is dealing with a new competitor from a developing country or problems obtaining a material necessary for their products. ARTT increases resiliency; you have a tool which allows you to work through problems and challenges and learn from whatever negative outcomes take place.

• Comfortable with paradox

Dealing effectively with paradox means you are able to hold two seemingly opposite concepts together in your mind. You've been told to cut staff, but increase your group's output. You need to concentrate on growing your people, but also must spend more time at the customer's office. It is possible to find ways to manage these paradoxical situations, but only if you are open-minded. If you have a rigid mindset—if you view things in black or white—then you are going to feel you need to choose one side of the paradox or the other. People on autopilot often see things from a narrow perspective; they've always focused on customer relationships so they decide they just don't have the time to develop their people. If you are using ARTT, however, you are much more likely to figure out a way to do both. You may not be able to achieve a perfect balance, but you evaluate each situation and determine when it would be best to focus on growing your people and when the customer must come first.

• Handles Complexity

Earlier we talked about being open to diverse ideas. Here, the goal is to synthesize a wide variety of information and opinions and arrive at an integrated conclusion. Leaders are being called upon to digest massive amounts of data and reach decisions with incredible speed. Becoming adept at integrating all this material makes it much easier to make sense of it. Instead of holding 100 different pieces of information in your mind, you can synthesize them into one clear concept or thesis. ARTT facilitates the type of uncluttered mind that can synthesize all this information rapidly. It helps clear away the emotional baggage from the past and lets people evaluate input cleanly and clearly.

• Leads by Example

ARTT is an action-oriented process. The Try part of the process requires leaders to do something rather than just think about it. This gives people the opportunity to test new leadership behaviors and determine which ones are effective. More so than ever before, people in organizations are cynical and skeptical about what leaders say. They want their bosses to walk the talk, and ARTT provides a way to help leaders do just that.

- **Respectful of Others**

When you are operating on autopilot, you are much more likely to be dismissive of others or at least be distanced from them. You are so wrapped up in your past emotional issues and related routines that you don't recognize your impact—or you fool yourself about that impact. The more in touch you are with what is going on in your head, the more perceptive you'll be about how you affect your direct reports, colleagues, bosses and customers. At a time when talent is increasingly scarce and relationships are the way to get things done, leaders must learn how to earn other people's trust. Treating them with dignity and respect are good ways to accomplish this objective.

The Need to Focus, to Gain Understanding, to Create Trust

These ten traits are not the only benefits of the ARTT process. As leaders find themselves increasingly strapped for time, with too much on their plates and trying to hold on to their best and brightest people, they need to be more focused, understanding and trustworthy than in the past. Let's look at each of these needs and see how ARTT helps meet them.

Focus is more important and more of a challenge than ever before. Leaders are faced with many choices and distractions, and it can be difficult to concentrate on mission-critical issues. Too often, we've seen leaders who have been caught up in minutia that they elevated into major issues. We've also seen leaders who have become enmeshed in pet projects and failed to concentrate on what really counts for their teams or organizations. When you are working 50 to 70 hour weeks, you can become so taxed trying to meet deadlines and satisfy demands that you may be involved with 10 projects at once. In reality, you should be concentrating on just one or two of those tasks.

As you recall, the Aware step of ARTT requires you to focus on "what" questions and become more aware of what is going on inside of you. With this higher awareness, you moved on to the Reflect step of the process and asked "why" questions: why are you obsessing about one issue when you might be thinking about something more important? This combination of grasping what is going on inside of you and why it matters allows you to focus. You gain insight into what you do throughout the day rather than just going through the motions. When you are on autopilot, your focus isn't sharp. When you turn it off and consider the "what" and "why" of your day, you are able to see yourself and your responsibilities with great clarity. This allows you to find the activity that requires your attention, making it your top priority.

Understanding is a broad term, but we're using it here to describe leaders' comprehension about what they're doing now versus what they need to do differently. It's very difficult for other people to articulate how a leader should change their behaviors to be more effective. While bosses and coaches can make good suggestions, they will never know you as well as you know yourself. Your boss can suggest that you would do a better job if you were better able to stick to deadlines, but that's just a surface goal. Using the Target step of ARTT, you can discover an area for improvement that is far more meaningful and challenging. Your Target emerges from intensive Awareness and Reflection, giving you insights no "outsider" can have. Leaders are being asked to make quantum leaps in performance—organizations have more ambitious goals that they'll never reach unless their leaders produce better results than in the past. Targeting the right area for improvement creates these quantum leaps.

All the self-deception that exists when someone is working on autopilot dissipates when they become highly conscious of their actions. The more in touch they get with their feelings and thoughts, the more they'll act out of a genuine sense of purpose rather than assume a pose that feels safe or they think is right for them. This is what is great about ARTT: the more you become self-aware and the more "natural" you act, the easier it is to gain trust.

Finally, leaders must be trusted if they are to succeed. People have too many options today and won't remain on the team of a leader they distrust. In fact, the very nature of teams—as opposed to the old hierarchical order that used to dominate most companies—requires leaders to communicate openly and honestly. Transparency is a prized quality in leaders, in large part because people trust leaders who lack hidden agendas. The ARTT process meets this trust need because it helps people act in more genuine ways.

The Lincoln Paradigm: What we can Learn about ARTT from our 16th President

Everyone knows that Abraham Lincoln was a great leader, but not everyone realizes that his greatness was due in part to his ability to coach himself with a process that seems similar (from our study of the literature about Lincoln) to ARTT. Of course, this term didn't exist back then, but from reading his various biographies, it becomes clear that he raised his personal Awareness level, Reflected, Targeted and Tried new behaviors.

As a young man, Lincoln had episodes of extreme depression, and he even had suicidal thoughts. At one point, he took aside a fellow state legislator and said, "I'm very much full of fun, and I know I seem like a vigorous fellow, but when I'm alone, I'm so full of mental depression that I won't even carry a knife in my pocket." One source of this depression was a series of painful memories.

In his book, *Lincoln's Melancholy*, Joshua Wolf Shenk reprints a letter Lincoln wrote to his law partner, including, "I am now the most miserable man living...To remain as I am is impossible. I must die or be better..."

Fortunately for him and for this country, he chose to be better. He learned how to cope and endure his life tragedies. He became highly conscious about his melancholy and depression, and found a way to apply the insights he gained. He established new routines that allowed him to rethink issues troubling him. When emotional pain or depression changed his behaviors, he would deal with these changes by writing letters; it was how he targeted areas where he needed to improve and thought about fresh actions he might take. He was very aware of both his thoughts and emotions, and he would take deliberate mental breaks to reflect on what was bothering him.

We're convinced that Lincoln became one of our best presidents because he was able to coach himself. Unlike many people during that era who were suffering from emotional traumas, Lincoln forced himself to be highly conscious and used this consciousness to change his behaviors.

Most great leaders we've observed possess *the Skill*, having used the basic steps of ARTT instinctively. That's how they become great. They don't allow traumatic experiences from their past to dictate how they respond to events in the present. They focus on what they are doing and why they are doing it, and in this way they can create a plan for change and improvement. And as we've pointed out, this change and improvement doesn't happen just once, but throughout their tenure as leaders. In this way, they continue to become more effective month by month and year by year.

ARTT may not be an instinctive method for you, but it can still be as effective as it is for any great leader. The key is practice. Make the four steps of ARTT your new routine. Make a conscious effort to cycle through them in a wide variety of work situations. As you move through the steps, focus on learning as much as you can and adapting your attitudes and behaviors based on that self-learning. You are not going to become Lincoln-esque overnight, but you'll see a definite evolution in your leadership abilities. Perhaps the first sign of a change will be your discovery that you can easily handle a situation that used to cause you problems. Or you'll find that your people are more responsive to your ideas and decisions. Or it may be that you start being contacted by headhunters or receiving job offers for top positions that never surfaced in the past.

Whatever the signs, you will find that ARTT enhances your performance, promotability and potential.

If you need any more motivation to embrace ARTT, then let me leave you with this last observation: as volatile as our current environment is, it is going to become even more volatile in the next decade. You are going to be asked to make more transitions than in the past, and they will certainly be more challenging. You may find yourself trying to manage a virtual team of people from different departments, countries and companies. You may be given a stretch assignment that demands you work faster and more innovatively than you ever have before. You may end up being transferred to a far corner of the world where you've never traveled, let alone worked.

To perform well in these unfamiliar, stressful circumstances, you're going to need some help. While it's great if you have a boss or a coach to assist you with these transitions, the truth is that no boss or coach is available consistently or when you need them most.

We've seen a wide range of business professionals meet huge challenges using ARTT, and we have great faith in its efficacy, and in your ability to maximize your potential.

SKILL SAVVY SUMMARY

THE LEADER: WHY ORGANIZATIONS WILL DEMAND HIGH PERFORMERS WHO CAN LEARN AND ADOPT

KEY POINTS

- The greatest predictors of leadership success are the abilities to learn from your experiences and be adaptable. *The Skill* is the tool-set that will give you access to these abilities.

The ARTT Diagram

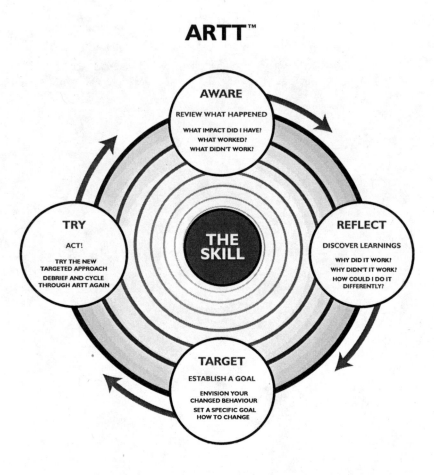

"My aim is to put down on paper what I see and what I feel in the best and simplest way."

— Ernest Hemingway

ACKNOWLEDGEMENTS

One of the most daunting, but rewarding tasks, is the challenge of acknowledging all those who helped this book become a reality -without leaving anyone out.

I first want to thank all my clients over the years, for their patience and faith in me, allowing me to evolve and practice the concepts that provided the basis for this book. I am grateful for Bruce Wexler as he was instrumental with his expertise, continuous sound advice and ability to keep us focused. I want to thank Amanda Regier for copy editing our material and Melanie Cooper for her assistance on the cover design. I want to express a heartfelt thanks to Dave Ulrich for taking the time to write a remarkable forward. In addition I would like to thank Ryan Benn, Randy White and Bill Frank for their willingness to give of their time and be a sounding board of sound advice.

I am indebted to Bob Eichinger for 25 years of professional mentoring and to Mike Lombardo for keeping me anchored in research. I would like to thank John Hirsch for his ongoing support and willingness to ask the discerning questions. Also, thanks to

Jon Martin Trondalen for his friendship and for greatly influencing my international perspective. And thanks to Lloyd Rindels
for his friendship over the years.

Lastly, I want to thank all of those, who over the years encouraged me to write a book.

Recommended Readings

Adams, Marilee G. *Change Your Questions, Change your Life: 7 Powerful Tools for Life and Work.* San Francisco: Berrett-Koehler, 2004.

Arbinger Institute. *Leadership and Self Deception: Getting out of the Box.* San Francisco: Berrett-Koehler, 2000.

Aryris, Chris. *Knowledge for Action.* San Francisco: Jossey-Bass, 1993.

Bandura, Albert. *Self-Efficacy: The Exercise of Control.* New York: Worth Publishers, 1997.

Bossidy, Larry and Ram Charan. *Confronting Reality: Doing What Matters to Get Things Right.* New York: Crown Business, 2004.

Ellis, Albert. *How to Control Your Anxiety Before It Controls You.* New York: Citadel, 2000.

Frankl, Vikto. *Man's Search for Meaning.* Boston: Beacon Press, 2006.

Gallwey, Timothy W. *The Inner Game of Work.* New York: Random House, 2000.

Goleman, Daniel. *Emotional Intelligence: Why It Can Matter More Than IQ.* New York: Bantam, 1995.

Hodgeson, Phillip and Randall White. *Relax, It's Only Uncertainty: Lead the Way While the Way is Changing.* New York: Pearson Press, 2001.

Ingram, Jay. *Theatre of the Mind: Raising the Curtain on Consciousness.* Toronto: Harper Collins, 2005.

Langer, Ellen J. *The Power of Mindful Learning.* New York: Perseus, 1997.

Latham, Gary. *Work Motivation: History, Theory, Research, and Practice.* London: Sage Publications, 2007.

Lombardo, Michael, Morgan Mccall and Ann Morrison. *The Lessons of Experience: How Successful Executives Develop on the Job.* Lexington Books, 1988.

Marquardt, Michael J. *Leading with Questions: How Leaders Find the Right Solutions by Knowing What to Ask.* San Francisco: Jossey-Bass, 2005.

Pink, Daniel H. *A Whole New Mind: Moving from the Information Age to the Conceptual Age.* New York: Penguin, 2005.

Schon, Donald A. *The Reflective Practitioner: How Professionals Think in Action.* New York: Basic Books, 1983.

Siegel, Daniel J. *The Mindful Brain: Reflection and Attunement in the cultivation of well-being.* New York: Mind Your Brain, Inc., 2007.

Smallwood, Norman and Dave Ulrich. *How Leaders Build Value: Using People, Organization , and other Intangibles to Get Bottom-Line Results.* New Jersey: Wiley, 2003.

ISBN 1425166199-9